Disabled Children:
Challenging Social Exclusion

Other titles in the series

Neglected Children: Issues and Dilemmas
O. Stevenson
0-632-04146-3

Introduction to Therapeutic Play
Jo Carroll
0-632-04148-X

Patterns of Adoption
D. Howe
0-632-04149-8

Family Group Conferences in Child Welfare
P. Marsh and G. Crow
0-632-04922-7

Young Carers and their Families
S. Becker, C. Dearden and J. Aldridge
0-632-04966-9

Child Welfare in the UK
Edited by O. Stevenson
0-632-04993-6

Also available from Blackwell Science

Child and Family Social Work
Editor: Professor David Howe
ISSN 1356-7500

Child and Family Social Work is a major international journal for all those concerned with the social and personal well-being of children and those who care for them. The Journal publishes original and distinguished contributions on matters of research, theory, policy and practice in the field of social work with children and their families. It aims to give international definition to the discipline and practice of child and family social work.

Child and Family Social Work is published quarterly

WORKING TOGETHER FOR CHILDREN,
YOUNG PEOPLE AND THEIR FAMILIES

SERIES EDITOR: PROFESSOR OLIVE STEVENSON

Disabled Children: Challenging Social Exclusion

Laura Middleton

Professor of Social Work, University of Central Lancashire

**Blackwell
Science**

© 1999 by
Blackwell Science Ltd
Editorial Offices:
Osney Mead, Oxford OX2 0EL
25 John Street, London WC1N 2BL
23 Ainslie Place, Edinburgh EH3 6AJ
350 Main Street, Malden
   MA 02148 5018, USA
54 University Street, Carlton
   Victoria 3053, Australia
10, rue Casimir Delavigne
   75006 Paris, France

Other Editorial Offices:

Blackwell Wissenschafts-Verlag GmbH
Kurfürstendamm 57
10707 Berlin, Germany

Blackwell Science KK
MG Kodenmacho Building
7–10 Kodenmacho Nihombashi
Chuo-ku, Tokyo 104, Japan

The right of the Author to be identified as
the Author of this Work has been asserted
in accordance with the Copyright, Designs
and Patents Act 1988

First published 1999

Set in 10/12 pt Sabon
by DP Photosetting, Aylesbury, Bucks
Printed and bound in Great Britain by
MPG Books Ltd, Bodmin, Cornwall

The Blackwell Science logo is a trade mark
of Blackwell Science Ltd, registered at the
United Kingdom Trade Marks Registry

DISTRIBUTORS

Marston Book Services Ltd
PO Box 269
Abingdon
Oxon OX14 4YN
(*Orders:* Tel: 01235 465500
         Fax: 01235 465555)

USA
Blackwell Science, Inc.
Commerce Place
350 Main Street
Malden, MA 02148 5018
(*Orders:* Tel: 800 759 6102
                781 388 8250
         Fax: 781 388 8255)

Canada
Login Brothers Book Company
324 Saulteaux Crescent
Winnipeg, Manitoba R3J 3T2
(*Orders:* Tel: 204 837 2987
         Fax: 204 837 3116)

Australia
Blackwell Science Pty Ltd
54 University Street
Carlton, Victoria 3053
(*Orders:* Tel: 03 9347 0300
         Fax: 03 9347 5001)

A catalogue record for this title
is available from the British Library

ISBN 0-632-05055-1

Library of Congress
Cataloging-in-Publication Data
is available

For further information on Blackwell
Science, visit our website:
www.blackwell-science.com

Contents

Foreword
by Professor Olive Stevenson

Laura Middleton has made in this book a valuable and timely contribution to our thinking about the position of disabled children in contemporary society. Politically, we hear much these days about attracting social exclusion and the damage it has done, particularly to children and young people. But, if this worthy objective is to be taken seriously, we have to acknowledge the diversity of the groups who may be described as excluded and within these the unique situations in which individuals may find themselves. The implication of that is that patient, detailed work in many different spheres is essential if we are to move towards a society which values and accepts all its members.

The author shows very clearly that, in relation to disabled children, we have a very long way to go. Indeed, the very concept of 'normalisation', which in some ways moved us on in our thinking, had negative consequences when it seemed to stress conformity rather than diversity. The ideal to which Laura Middleton aspires is a society which includes and values diversity of all kinds. Hence, for example, her emphasis on the right of disabled children to be fully integrated into mainstream schools.

For policy makers, such a determined stance may pose problems in terms of competing demands for resources. However, as the author points out, behind the real obstacles to, and tensions in, making appropriate provision across a range of services, there lie deeper resistances which reflect the ambivalence we feel about people who are different and whose impairments make us feel uncomfortable. In this context, the first and fourth chapters illuminate the issues particularly well.

The book is written with a strong sense of the injustice towards disabled children which is perpetuated in so many ways and shows the powerful impact on our thinking which the 'social model' of disability has had. But for those in practice, it is worth remembering that we have come a remarkably long way in recent years. The irony is that books like this reflect a general growth in awareness and sensitivity – a culture in which such ideas can be taken seriously.

There seem to me to be three prerequisites for further progress. First, a personal, professional and political commitment to the principle of social inclusion; second, an extension of empathy so that the position and feelings of disabled children are better understood. Thirdly, there has to be a refusal to put people and problems into bureaucratic boxes, rigid categories which impoverish opportunity and provision. (A contemporary example is the way in which disabled children have not been adequately included in child protection systems.)

The approach of this book will be welcomed by many committed practitioners who are working in this field. It renews the sense of urgency.

Olive Stevenson
Professor Emeritus of Social Work Studies

Preface

I had a conversation recently with a PhD student, who was working on the social exclusion of young people. To my dismay, she told me she was not including disabled children in her study. In answer to my somewhat incredulous 'Why not?', she replied that they were 'excluded anyway', as if their exclusion was somehow natural, acceptable and immutable. Sadly she is not alone. Service providers from both health and social services often make statements to the effect that child protection swallows all the resources and leaves nothing for disabled children, without apparently noticing the illogicality of the remark. This kind of thinking is made possible because of the conceptual separation we are able to make between 'children' and 'disabled children'. As a result education, health and welfare can operate services on a different basis for children labelled as 'disabled'.

While to some people, including myself, this separation may simply seem inherently wrong, a more objective approach is to enquire whether or not it causes any actual harm. This exploration takes place in the context of current European concern with social exclusion: a concept initially relating to employment practices, but which has been widened to address the ways in which children and adults are denied opportunities within mainstream society. The more rigidly lines are drawn around what is 'normal', the more people and groups will be excluded. It follows that the best way to achieve social inclusion is to expand the boundaries of society to allow more diversity.

I am therefore looking for the answer to a key question : what is the justification for treating disabled children differently?

This question is addressed from different perspectives; not only those of the different professionals who deal with disabled children, but, centrally, those of the children concerned : patients, pupils, clients or service users. In seeking this consumer viewpoint, I approached disabled students from the University of Central Lancashire to discuss their childhood experiences with me. Happily, they were more than willing (see Appendix 1 for details). These interviews explore what difference having a physical disability made to the students in their relationships with family, friends, schools and professional helpers, and helped to determine the content of the rest of the book.

Starting with the views of young people does not mean professional or parental perspectives are insignificant, but is an acknowledgement that the child's view may have been less influential than others in developing the services which we currently have. The second chapter explores whether disadvantage for disabled children is created in service provision, looking at evidence from health, education and social services. The analysis brings together two sets of information, the first concerning the children's experience and development and the second concerning effects of disability. This is still a relatively unusual perspective. While there is a great deal of academic and professional literature about childcare and about disability, there is comparatively little which combines the two, except in the field of education.

If the current pattern of separate services cannot be justified, then ways must be sought to do things differently in the future. This means addressing some uncomfortable possibilities: might we be placing organisational and professional needs ahead of those of the children concerned? Is it easier to contract out services than expect all of our staff to develop an understanding of the needs of disabled children? Is maintaining a separate identity a way of keeping the issue on the agenda? This argument justifies specialist teams everywhere, and means playing a dangerous game between catering for particular needs which might otherwise be unmet, and maintaining segregation because it becomes administratively and professionally convenient.

Chapter Three looks at some of the conceptual frameworks involved in change, and Chapters Four and Five offer suggestions for how changes might be effected personally, professionally and organisationally. In considering such changes, the sensitivities of professional staff who are doing their best under difficult circumstances have to be understood. Similarly if the analysis suggests greater attention could be paid to children's priorities, ways have to be found to adjust that balance while remaining fair to parents. We are all caught in the same web.

But it is even more complicated than that. If change followed naturally from reasoned argument, changing the world would be easy. Any attempt to make a difference for marginalised groups has to develop from an understanding of why those in possession of power choose to exclude. My ideas about this in relation to disabled children form the final part of the book, and in Chapter Six I suggest some ways in which the rules which govern our social and societal relationships might be changed.

The astute reader may point out that, in promoting the ideal of inclusion and then concentrating on a single group of children, this book carries an essential contradiction. I have argued that separation requires justification. There has, therefore, to be a good reason to write a book about disabled children, given the wealth of literature which already exists on childcare, children's health, education and child protection. My justification is that many writers on childcare have not included issues as they affect *all* children, including those who are disabled, in their analysis. This book may make a contribution to the ideal of social justice by placing disabled children within the mainstream of contemporary debates.

Acknowledgements

This book could not have been written without the generosity and support of others. The credit for talking me into it goes to Janie Thomas and I hope she approves of the result. Many people, both academics and practitioners, gave me helpful advice, pointers, previews and /or permission to use their material. In particular, I would like to thank Colin Barnes, Ruth Eley, Sally French, Ann Gegg, Phillip Graves, Kamlesh Patel, Mark Priestley, Ann Ridgeway and Tom Shakespeare. The staff in the Disabled Students Resource Unit at the University of Central Lancashire put me in touch with disabled students and provided interpreting services.

I am grateful to all the students who gave so generously of their time in sharing their experiences and to Joanne Hill who conducted the interviews with enthusiasm and sensitivity. The students all appear under pseudonyms in the main script, and unless respondents specifically asked to be named in person I have retained their anonymity. Those who agreed to a personal acknowledgement are: Christine Brolughan, Michelle Cunningham, William Graham, Angus Huntley, Asif Iqbal, Dave Kinela, Jane Titherington, Shazia Ullah, Christopher Wainman and Susan Williams. I would also like to thank Dr and Mrs Awbery-Taylor for permission to use extracts from Jason's autobiography.

Above all, I have been more than fortunate in my friends. Ruth Eley, Ann Gegg, Agnes Tomlinson and Gail Tucker all kept me going, one way or another, during what proved to be a difficult year. Finally, my thanks are due to Olive Stevenson, for her kindness and hospitality, as well as for her patient and rigorous editing.

Laura Middleton
1998

Chapter 1

Children's Voices: Hopes, Wishes and Dreams

'40c in the slot for the handicapped children of the Blue Mountains will speak the legend'.

Three Sisters Fountain, New South Wales

Traditional explanations of disadvantage experienced by disabled children rest on the medical model of disability which holds that the trauma of impairment is in itself an explanation for the individual's failure to achieve a reasonable quality of life. The 'social model' shifts this emphasis away from pathologising the individual and stresses restrictive environments and attitudes.

If this model of disability has any validity at all, it must mean that a disabled child experiences childhood differently from a non disabled child. But are their hopes, wishes and dreams any different? The young people interviewed for this book did not dream great dreams or entertain vaulting ambitions for themselves, but they did have ideas about their futures. What happened to their hopes? The stories in this chapter may not constitute conclusive evidence about the careers of all children with physical impairments, but for those willing to listen and wishing to effect change, there is more than enough material to indicate the direction such changes should be taking.

This does not simply involve finding ways to make things better, but also entails identifying and addressing the ways in which we make things worse: how professionals and organisations disable children.

This chapter describes childhood experiences which were neither extreme nor worst case scenarios, derived from interviews with disabled students (see Appendix 1). These represent an articulate and successful group of young people whose childhoods have three key things in common:

- Firstly, they all had a physical impairment of some kind.
- Secondly, all of them experienced damaging reactions and behaviours from other children, from adults and from members of the caring professionals. These were not necessarily, nor even usually, intentionally malicious. Indeed, some were thought to be helpful behaviours.

- Thirdly, all the respondents attributed most of the negative experiences in their lives to their physical impairments, directly or indirectly. It was their impairments which dominated and gave meaning to their explanations of what had happened to them.

Families

In his autobiography Jason Awbery-Taylor tells a story about being taken home by his non-disabled school-friend to meet his friend's parents for the first time (see Appendix 1). They were clearly shocked to see Jason was in a wheelchair. Despite relaying all kinds of other personal information about his new friend to his parents, including the sort of food he would appreciate for tea, the young host had not thought it necessary to mention that his guest could not walk. This may say a great deal about the respective concerns of adults and children.

Most respondents reported times when they felt their parents overprotected them:

> 'As a child I was never left alone apart from bedtime. I wanted to be left alone. Even going to the toilet somebody had to sit me on the toilet and wait for me to get off. That scared me because I didn't want people round me all the time.'

Most of the students in the survey had non-disabled parents, which meant they lacked personal experience of the disabling condition and were not always able to provide sound advice to their children. Parents can feel de-skilled by disabilities particularly if they remain surrounded in medical mystique. Billy was sympathetic with parents.

> 'They don't have the experience. That's why they fumble about in the dark for so long',

while another student had some advice :

> 'I would encourage hearing parents of a deaf child to meet other parents of deaf children, deaf parents as well, to support each other and don't think of the child as a medical problem'.

In the absence of personal experience or sound professional advice or help, some parents may turn to other sources of support such as religion. This can result in a fatalistic perspective, but it is an attempt to find a reason where there may be none:

> 'My Mom says that if you have a disability you are selected. Most people have to cope only with normality, whereas I have been selected to cope with something extra.'

Disabled children were often treated differently from their siblings, sometimes to protect them. Brothers and sisters were allowed to play outside, visit friends, and attend youth clubs while the disabled young people were kept at home.

'That made me really moody because I wanted to go with boys'.

Sometimes differential treatment reflected a desire to compensate but it had unhelpful effects. One student reported that his sister always got smacked but that he never did; even when he stole from shops he was 'always Mummy's boy'. This different treatment caused friction with his sister. Another reflected with hindsight that always being allowed 'a seat about three feet from the television' made him lazy and his brothers angry.

Only one respondent reported that his family took the opposite approach and made vigorous efforts not to treat him differently:

'They even came out with stuff like: "for God's sake, Billy, are you blind?"'

All children lack experience. Disabled children grow up having to make sense of the world around them in the context of their impairment, and yet non-disabled parents and other adults may not be in a position to interpret, understand or advise. However empathetic they may be, non-disabled adults cannot really ever *know* what it is like to see as their child sees, hear how they hear, walk with a calliper or have limited control over an unruly tongue. As a result, children may find themselves afraid, isolated, misunderstood or constantly having to explain.

'It's difficult having to explain your deafness and special needs all the time. Some of the lecturers have a negative attitude. One even offered for me to tape record his lecture!'

I have come across such inappropriate responses to sensory impairment before, particularly in confusing the effects of deafness and visual impairment. Most people who make such remarks or take unhelpful actions are embarrassed once these are pointed out. That it happens does not demonstrate stupidity so much as unfamiliarity and an eagerness to help. I can vividly remember a keen instructor at a PHAB club embarrassing himself in front of a group of young people by offering a deaf boy who was on his first visit there the loan of a football with a bell in it: a piece of equipment supplied by the Leisure Centre for blind players. Even more vivid, sadly, is the memory of the deaf young man who could see that everyone was laughing but had no idea why.

Often parents are having to learn new skills at the same time as their child and may be more self conscious about it:

'My Mum has learnt and passed levels one and two in sign language but she won't sign to me.'

False assumptions were made by parents about the nature of disability and what it might mean, the most common being that disabled children would not develop normally: go through puberty, be capable of sexual intercourse, or become parents themselves. This belief about the per-petual childhood of disabled children has meant that they were often kept in ignorance about sex and sexuality.

> 'When I started my periods I stayed in the toilet all day. I thought I was dying. All my Mum said was you will have to watch the boys now. I didn't know ~~what she meant.~~'

While the student above believed that her mother had made wrong assumptions about what her disability meant, being kept in ignorance about sexual relationships is not necessarily related to disability. The young people who made these and earlier comments on parental pressure and protection attributed their ignorance and their relation-ship difficulties to their disability. Professionals often fail to do any-thing to explain how normal these experiences are. However, ignorance of sex is increasingly anachronistic and disabled young people may lie in some danger of becoming isolated from their peer group, as well as more vulnerable to abuse, if for whatever reason parents treat them as perpetual children.

Most of the respondents did have sexual experience, sometimes as children, giving the lie to the myth that disabled children are not sexual beings. Nor were they embarrassed about indulging in some boasting about it, sometimes at the expense of their parents:

> 'I lost my virginity when I was 14 with a lad from the youth club. He was very good. When I was 15 my dad said he had better have a word with me. He was very red.'

Becoming sexually active is taken as a sign of adulthood, and this group of students very much wanted to belong. Nevertheless, sexual experi-ence in ignorance of the facts can be dangerous. Residential schools offer excellent opportunities for sexual encounters, which may not be matched with proper safeguards in terms of information about con-traception or hygiene:

> 'When you go to college it's all full of partially sighted and blind kids all bed hopping.'

As an additional complication, this student noted the high incidence of genetic conditions within his school, carrying the danger not only of unwanted teenage pregnancy but of passing on disabling genes. All of the above demonstrate the dangers of keeping children in ignorance about sex, relationships and the nature of their own conditions.

Making friends

Most of the students reported difficulties getting to know people, which they attributed to their own difference. One student described feeling it was 'like me against the world'. People's initial sympathy turned to hostility when she did not conform to their expectations of a disabled person: a problem she exacerbated by frustrated tantrums. A blind student described how having a guide dog had helped as it 'tends to break the ice a bit. People will talk to the dog.' This did not always result in conversation as 'sometimes they *just* talked to the dog,' which offended him. While not wishing to deny the unease many people experience in talking with someone with whom they cannot make eye contact, the willingness of many children and adults who are uneasy with other people to converse with animals, or even soft toys, is well known and understood. This fact could helpfully have been discussed with the student as part of his training as a guide dog user, and might have enabled him to take people's behaviour less personally.

Lack of experience of disabled and non-disabled people meeting each other is one direct result of a segregated educational system, which creates an atmosphere of mutual fear and potential for misunderstanding.

'I know people are dubious about approaching me and speaking because they automatically see blindness first, but they don't seem to realise it's just as difficult for me to go to you and speak to you.'

While non-disabled people may find themselves reacting with unease toward disabled people, the students who grew up in segregated schools reported feelings such as isolation and nervousness. They were well aware that non-disabled people 'imagine that a conversation with a disabled person is going to be difficult'. Meeting new people can make anyone feel nervous, but the disabled students believed their education made it difficult 'to fit into a wider society'. They saw themselves as different and marginalised, so much so that non-disabled people were described by the term 'normal'.

'When I was at (special school) I would get excited if a normal person walked in.'

Making assumptions based on physical characteristics is not uncommon. Blind people have been attributed with special powers. They are often stereotyped as very musical and have been assigned the gift of prophesy, or the inner eye. On the other hand they are said to need help crossing the street. None of these preconceptions about difference help communication. Confidence can quickly be undermined. Ayesha Vernon describes her experience on her first day in a mainstream college of education where the warden of the residential hall told her she had a double handicap of colour and blindness and that most of the other students had experience of neither. She took that as meaning she would not make friends there.

'Before that fatal comment which dashed my confidence to pieces in a flash, I had already met and thought I had made some friends, but after that I kept myself to myself and focused my attention on my studies which I saw as the key to my liberation.'

(Vernon, 1996 p 50)

Hamida also found making friends daunting, and blamed the other children's reaction to her disability. She was ignored by fellow pupils who refused to sit next to her, work with her on assignments, and called her unpleasant names which implied that she was stupid and smelly. These are common children's insults but Hamida believed it was her disability which created the animosity.

The students nearly all shared the perception that adults saw them as stupid: 'people think we are dead from the neck up and the waist down'. Adults who shouted on the assumption that the students could not hear or understand were not uncommon. This tendency to attribute lack of ability to them was a more serious problem than the disabling conditions themselves:

'I'm not really so bothered any more whether I can see or not. The main problem is people who automatically think that you're thick or just doubt your ability.'

On the other hand, some of the pressures created for disabled people are not always well understood and behaviours may be misinterpreted as a result.

'I don't look at people's faces when I'm travelling because I've fallen out of the wheelchair several times because I'm not looking where I'm going. So now I stare at the floor.'

The chances are that someone meeting her staring at the floor would not assume she was scared but decide she was being antisocial or was intellectually impaired.

Donald also reported staring at the floor.

'I was scared quite a lot as a child of kerbs as well as of the dark and of spiders. I look down because I'm looking out for potholes. I suppose it looks ignorant but I've got to do it.'

Children with impairments are made to feel embarrassed by them and dislike 'people drawing attention to it'. One boy kept his hands in his pockets because they were misshapen. This was taken as rudeness by more than one adult. Feeling different left many of the students feeling miserable or embarrassed, which can develop into shyness, loneliness, a fear of getting close to others or antisocial behaviour. For one woman this turned into seriously disturbed behaviour which, had she been able bodied, would almost certainly have resulted in a referral for professional help, rather than being ignored as part of the disabling condition:

'I went through a phase of making weird moaning noises in shops and rolling my head about. Nobody spoke to me then.'

The origins of embarrassment lie in the reactions of other people to impairments, indicating that they constitute a source of shame or are something to be mocked. This is learned behaviour. Babies are not born feeling embarrassed about themselves or parts of themselves. Nor do children naturally feel embarrassed about the impairments they see in others, although they may be curious.

I well remember coming up behind my nine-year-old nephew and his friend, who walked using a Piedro boot and calliper, and over-hearing a very frank and open discussion about the latter's 'bad leg', which was conducted without a hint of embarrassment on either part. I was left wondering how we lose such ability to communicate as adults.

> 'Kids are so honest all the time and not diplomatic at all. They just come out with things. My brother as a kid said to me: "Why don't you live with us?" and I've just said, that it's because my eyes don't work like yours do. The parents feel embarrassed more than the kids do.'

Such inhibitions develop as children get older and can make both helping and receiving help a potential minefield.

> 'She, this friend of mine, can actually get a strop on with people who offer to help, which is fair enough, and she has a right to do that, but I think she'd be better off saying "No thank you, I'm all right".'

> 'When I first started here it used to really crush my soul, I'd have to ask everyone to open the door. And I've got this thing now where I just say "Can you get that door for us, cheers, thanks" and I don't even know when I'm saying it. I don't even mean it. I don't even look at them because I do it so often.'

While you could argue that automatic doors would solve the access problem, they would not help with the underlying relationship diffi-culty which is reflected time and time again in interactions between disabled and non-disabled people. Some twenty years ago, as a student in a residential home for disabled people, I had adopted a philosophy of not helping unless I was asked to do so. It was the heyday of 'inde-pendent living' and I had no wish to patronise anyone. This plan worked fine until the day I was very busily propping up a radiator while watching a young disabled woman encumbered with sticks and her shopping struggling to negotiate a heavy door.

> 'What's up with you?' she shouted angrily, 'Do you think I'm bloody bionic or something?'

It taught me that it was as naive not to offer to help a disabled person as it was not to offer help to anyone else I encountered who might wel-come assistance. Inexperience of each other has complicated the normal helping relationships that are conducted between people on a day-to-day basis. It has made some disabled people angry, and it is fear of encountering such anger that makes many potential helpers keep their distance.

Donald suggested compelling able-bodied people to sit in a wheel-chair for a week 'for *their* education, and *my* vengeance.' He did not mind that they would only be pretending, since they would face the same problems if only for that short length of time.

> 'They would still be sitting at the bottom of the stairs thinking, how do I get up this?'

Other relationship problems arise because of the fear of standing out in crowds. Having a visible disabling condition makes it less easy to blend into the background on those occasions which can make people feel uncomfortable. One respondent described the fears he had about a family wedding. This even came down to the fact that he might 'make the photographs look stupid'.

This story reflects a common mixture among the students of low self esteem and an acute, arguably unhealthy preoccupation with bodily image. This may be a result of the excessive concentration many of them experienced during childhood and adolescence on their body and its imperfections.

> 'The professionals concentrated almost entirely on my disability. Limbs had to be straightened and exercised, physiotherapy and walking were priorities while mentally and emotionally I was stagnating.'

Barron describes how the everyday lives of disabled girls and women involve a great deal of physiotherapy treatment which aims at 'cor-recting' and 'making whole' their bodies. They learn from an early age that their bodies need 'repair', and are therefore not 'normal' (Barron, 1997). Many learn not to have a positive approach to their bodies as a result.

It is also worth remembering that many disabled children do not meet *disabled* adults and lack positive role models as a result. Cindy described how she felt meeting a disabled adult for the first time:

> 'I don't know what I thought happened to disabled people but I can remember being surprised to see a disabled adult with make up and fags and just conducting herself in a very adult way'.

It was both sad and salutary to note that many of the participants were unable to generalise with any ease beyond their own personal experi-ences of disability. This self-centredness was even more understandable when life expectancy was poor:

> 'Actually I get a bit selfish and I think, well, why do I have to do this because I have more important things on my mind, like am I going to live to see 25 sort of thing. Why do I have to stress out about a stupid essay that's got no relevance at all. And at other times you think well if you didn't stress about those things then you wouldn't be living a life properly would you?'

'It chips away at you inside': the experience of bullying

Bullying of younger children by older children is common, reflecting obvious power differences. The targeting of disabled children as unable to retaliate is a similar imbalance, and was widely noticed: 'They used to think it's OK. Hit him and run because he can't catch you.' Disabled children are belittled, bullied, and abused. Despite the fact that the research was not specifically looking for bullied or abused children, numerous examples of such behaviour were noted.

> 'We had to wear those really big hearing aids and the hearing boys used to come up behind us and pull the backs off them which caused them to bang on our chins.'

This is not to suggest that disabled children were simply victims. Disabled children, like others, may react to bullying by giving as good as they get, moving the behaviour down the pecking order. This was frequently noted by students with visual impairments. There seems to be a particularly strong sense of hierarchy between blind and partially-sighted children.

> 'It's very strange, even at a visually impaired school it's the blind students are one section and the partially-sighted are another and they don't integrate.'

Nor was bullying confined to minor injury or insult.

> 'There was this seventeen-year-old deaf lad who put a five-year-old deaf lad's arm in the door and closed it, and broke it in four places.'

A blind student reported being kicked in the head by a group of deaf boys to whom he refused to give a football.

Bullying is used to reinforce power differences based on age, intelligence and perceived normality: the more intelligent pupils 'always basically mocked the ones that were obviously less intelligent or less able'. It was easier to join in the system.

> 'I am ashamed to say that I am guilty of some bullying of my own. I remember being very intolerant of children with poorer sight than myself.'

Bullying does not simply relate to disability but to difference. In one special school it was religion which set a victim apart:

> 'There was this lad who was a lot bigger than me at school, he always picked on me. For a year he picked on me: he called me a "wee shit" this and a "wee Catholic that", and he would punch me and stuff.'

Nor was it just boys who were bullies, although girls may use different techniques. The results can be equally serious: 'It got so bad the girl became anorexic'. Such psychological pressure may be more difficult to identify and deal with than direct physical abuse.

Becoming a bully oneself does not erase the pain:

> 'People used to say "you can be really nasty sometimes" and that's probably true. I did it to get my own back, but it chips away at you inside.'

It was nonetheless recognised by one respondent that not dealing with the situation could have dire long term consequences:

> 'You'll end up in a huddled mess sitting in a corner crying your eyes out with your thumb in your mouth when you're 33 years old.'

Hamida's situation is more complex. The bullying she reported distressed her particularly because it came from within her own community.

> 'It wasn't English people who bullied me it was Asian people like myself, not just because I couldn't talk but also they thought I looked ugly. They would pick on me because of that, and my clothes, on my speech.'

Her unhappiness manifested itself in a shocking way. She reacted to the bullying by trying to change her appearance in the belief that things would be better for her if she looked different.

> 'I did stupid things, like I rubbed my face with floor cleaner to make myself whiter. I cut my hair, I cut chunks off the front. There was one time I was so unhappy I got a knife and cut myself.'

Teenagers who self abuse are not uncommon, nor is it unusual to hear of black children who attempt to turn themselves white. Professional helpers have to recognise that these difficulties also affect disabled children.

The ability to learn to cope owes a great deal to family and social circumstances. Billy was proud of his resilience which he attributed to the nature of his community:

> 'The way I was brought up, you get stick like everyone else does, and you learn to cope with it or learn to fight back and you would be fighting physically or just giving verbal abuse and that's the way it was because that's the environment I grew up in. Whereas a lot of the special kids that I encountered couldn't handle stick because they'd been so isolated all their lives.'

Billy moved from mainstream to special education when he was fifteen. He believed the children in residential school had less ability to cope with bullying than he had developed in mainstream, where if someone bullied him he could simply hit back or get his brother to do it for him. Such solutions are less easily available in residential settings. Children away from home are not only physically separated from support, but may also feel that their parents care less about what happens to them. This does not apply solely to disabled children, but is a feeling they will share with many children in public school. Sharon was one of the few respondents to recognise that the problems lay not with her disability but having to live away from home. She missed her family and had difficulties fitting back in when she left school, having become detached from family life because she could not keep up with what was going on there.

These experiences illustrate two key points. First, that problems for a disabled child can be compounded by being sent away from home; and second, that, even if we found ways to keep residential care free of abuse, it would still remain a poor choice.

The fact that parents may believe that they are doing the right thing educationally does not alter the perception of being uncared for either by the child, or by any potential abuser. Lack of family and community support makes it easier – both practically and psychologically – for staff to engage in abusive behaviour.

Adult abusers

It is not only children who bully. Some professional carers indulge in abusive behaviour which uses the child's impairment as a source of fun. Respondents reported that staff employed to help with personal care made jokes out of it.

'They used to call me a dunce because I walked funny. They really used to pick on me. They said I was only good for one thing: your leg over.'

The sadistic gym teacher is perhaps more widely recognisable:

'One teacher I hated. He was bawling "get up the ropes" you know. I said "well I can't, can I? Look at me!'. I just sulked in a corner.'

Since it would be easy to behave differently, one is forced to the conclusion that some people enjoy humiliating children. The respondents' ideas of what would have constituted helpful behaviour do not require a great deal of skill or extra resources: but they do require attitudinal change. They wanted teachers to be nice; to enquire whether or not they could manage, and how they felt.

'It would just reassure you somebody is a bit concerned about you.'

They suggested much stronger disciplinary procedures for those teachers who abused them, and for those who let it happen.

Neglect and incompetence were also reported in schools. In two cases this related to careless treatment by school nurses; both of these demonstrate an inattention to the possibility that disabled children may have other medical conditions. One concerned a blind student who 'fell asleep for two days and then they found she had diabetes'. In another case, a child whose leg was broken in a fall was treated with aspirin.

Some respondents reported much more serious instances of abuse. In so small a sample, in which we were not specifically looking for respondents who had experienced abuse, they stand out as powerful testimony, albeit anecdotal, to the levels of abuse within our educational system. These involved both corporal punishment and sexual abuse. There have been sufficient reported incidents of abuse in residential care in the last few years for its potential danger not to need labouring here, except to point out that such abuse is not confined to able bodied children.

Failure to protect

Not only do adults bully, and arguably set the tone for bullying, they also manifestly fail to protect, or even be aware of what is happening. Signs of distress were ignored. One student pretended he was ill because of the mocking he experienced at school. Dinner and play breaks are times at which children are particularly vulnerable. Respondents felt staff either failed to notice, or dealt inadequately with the bullies when they did.

'The lads that beat me up just lost their lunch break privileges for two days.'

Two quotes from Randall's book on bullying further illustrate how cruelly difference can be picked on by children, and how inadequate schools seem to be in countering it (Randall, 1997). The first case had been going on for years unchecked, and even worse, the second illustrates how a direct cry for help from a child went unheeded:

'As soon as they found out I couldn't see very well, they started taking my things and hiding them. It's been going on for years now. When I start looking they sing "Bottle Bottom's on the trail again" and slap me with rulers.'

(9-year-old in an independent school) (p 10)

'My deformed spine makes me all bent over and doubled up. Some of the girls started calling me "Quasy" after the Hunchback, then they started saying my father buggers me standing up. I complained to the teacher but she thought I was lying.'

(14 year old boy in a mixed comprehensive) (p 11)

Rather than receiving help to understand or address the structural issues around discrimination or bullying, the respondents found themselves pathologised as in need of psychiatric help. One respondent was under five at the time, and his parents were advised that disabled children went through 'phases'.

There is a frightening dearth of help for disabled youngsters. None of the respondents experienced any form of help to manage bullying or to deal with discrimination until and unless they redefined themselves as 'ill' or 'depressed'. A number of the respondents had done this as young adults. Hamida cut herself as a result of bullying having 'just bottled things up for about 11 years'. By the time problems came to light, it was the students themselves who were seen as the source, rather than the adversity of their situations. As a result, they could become labelled as difficult or in need of psychiatric help. Another reported:

> 'They took me in a room and asked me what was going on. They offered to refer me to a psychiatrist but I wouldn't go. They thought I was loopy but I was not.'

Nor were parents always aware of what was happening, or able to deal with it. This meant they could easily get the blame for the child's unhappiness:

> 'I would come out with some horrible things, like telling my mother I wish she'd never had me ... did she think about *my* life? She didn't take it very well.'

Growing up in care: Alice's story

One of the respondents, Alice, was brought up in local authority residential care and foster homes from the age of six months, as was her older brother. They were not always together, and contact with her natural mother was sporadic. She was 20 years old at the time of the interview, so her experiences in the care system are recent. Despite the fact that Alice was the only respondent who was brought up in care, her story contains messages that are relevant for anyone with an interest in improving service provision. Alice felt different from other children not so much because of her disability, but because she was not with her own family.

Her relationship with her mother and brother was regulated by social services. There were reviews twice a year in the children's home during which Alice maintained that she wanted to retain contact with her mother, whom she missed. She believed her mother felt the same way:

> 'She's lost contact with another child that was adopted before my brother and I were born, and I think she was always worried that she was going to lose us.'

Alice was subjected to a range of ideological influences, as she moved from residential to foster homes, and as she changed school, which make her childhood read more like a Dickens novel than an enlightened child care system.

> 'It was a Catholic school and I'm not a religious person. The school forced religion onto people. They were quite strict.'

Her foster mother grew organic vegetables and had strong opinions about chemicals in food. She told Alice she was overweight and refused to let her have milk in her tea. Breakfast cereal was served with orange juice on. Alice blamed this regime for giving her a complex about her appearance. She was also forbidden to play pop music or have posters in her room. As if this were not enough she was also physically abused.

'We went to the beach one day and we came back and she said oh, you haven't been to the toilet all day, and I said I didn't really want to go, and she said before I could have something to eat, you should go. When I said I didn't think I could she ended up slapping me around the face.'

Social work review visits to the foster home were not helpful, although Alice anticipated them for weeks ahead:

'She didn't know how much I worked myself up about her visit. I was just miserable, I felt so isolated. My foster mother just dictated what I did.'

Alice believed the social worker had the power to influence her situation, but failed to take the necessary action.

An eventual move to a children's home did not solve the isolation problem since by this time Alice was perceived as a hard-to-manage child. The other children in the home were a transient population of boys in trouble with the police, making it an unstable environment. The staff also changed a great deal, although Alice clearly preferred them to her foster carers:

'They were actually very nice, but the thing that I found difficult was that it would be a different person on duty every day and I always used to feel upset that it was somebody who looked after me that was paid to do it not because they loved me. That used to hurt quite a lot.'

Education

All the respondents reported that they were expected to achieve less than their non-disabled contemporaries. They felt themselves written off and uncared for. Videos were widely used as a substitute for including children in lessons, and teaching staff were variously reported as uncaring, embarrassed, mocking and ignorant. Dreams were squashed without any obvious attempts either to find ways to realise them or to offer reasonable alternatives:

'When I was young I wanted to be a geologist, you know, dinosaurs and stuff because I was really interested in it. But as I got older I became aware of my being in a wheelchair, and it dawned on me it wouldn't be possible.'

'When I left school they had my parents and myself in the office and they said I would never be an academic.'

This second quotation comes from a student with cerebral palsy who did not learn to read until her early twenties. During her years in special education, no-one had realised that in addition to her obvious motor problems, which were treated with vigour, she also had extremely poor eyesight.

Most of the respondents had fought off the image of stupidity, but the process left them feeling angry:

'I don't consider myself disabled generally, but people who are disabled are taught that to be like a normal person you've got to be better qualified because you've got to work ten times harder and fight ten times harder to get to the same position. I just thought to myself, no I'm not stupid. It's just that I was told all my life I was stupid and I thought , 'No, stuff them.'

Sharon wrote to me that the staff at the mainstream school she attended for a year when aged five were instructed not to teach her to read, on the grounds that her new school would probably teach her in a different way. Expectation is relative, of course. In Simon's case a successful career meant being able to get a place at the colliery in the small mining community where:

'Everyone knew everyone else: my early education, if you can call it that, sitting at the back of the classroom and being given crayons to play with due to my sight problem. I do not know if this was deliberate discrimination or just, why teach someone who could not work down the pit and would end up with a menial job anyway?'

A move to a special school across the Pennines did not help, and actually increased his problems by moving him out of a close knit community where he felt 'safe and secure'. Even children who demonstrate ability at school may be directed away from mainstream opportunities into specialist colleges. Despite being considered bright enough to continue their education, choices were limited to

'Hereford College, a college of FE for disabled youth; Fourways, a training centre for disabled in Wigan, or there was the National Star Centre.'

Special schools, in particular, were criticised for not placing education at the top of their priority list,

'Concentrating not on my academic side, not even my speech. They were concentrating on trying to get me to walk.'

A common feeling was that too much emphasis was placed on correcting the physical deficiencies at the expense of recognising and developing things that could be done:

'Nobody is pushed to the limits, even the people that may be more able, they're still not pushed to their potential. You're just left.'

This resulted in children leaving school without any qualifications, despite the fact that all the respondents later went on to demonstrate their ability to pursue degree-level study. Even in the one case where a special school provided education up to GCSE, it meant the pupils sacrificing a year, so that a perfectly normal experience became abnormal. Respondents also noted that there appeared to be less accountability where poor standards existed in special education. One reported being taught maths by someone who had actually failed his own A-level and whose only qualification was as a typist:

> 'Everyone knew what Mr. B. did but nobody did anything. He sat and smoked in class and drank coffee, and if I was good he'd let me fill his flask full of hot water for him. I did it just to prove to myself that I was good for something. It can happen a lot more in special education.'

School inspections failed to help and were regarded by pupils as 'sham'. The inspectors did not speak to the children and the staff were perceived as playing to the gallery: 'They probably did more work that day than they did the whole year'. This lack of rigour was reported as a feature of special schools and reinforces the students' view that these schools did not place academic achievement very high on their agendas, nor was there evidence that outside regulation placed any such expectations on them.

Moving to special school during childhood was experienced by several respondents as without choice, and as a retrograde step. In particular it meant loss of friends.

> 'Coming away from home, leaving all your friends behind, leaving your family, and sitting in a place where you don't know anyone and you're completely depressed and all you want to do is go home.'

Some respondents were unclear why they needed to go at all.

> 'I wasn't very good at walking but I could still walk. I think it was just the mentality that if there was anything up with anyone they would just send them to special school.'

One thought his parents were

> 'Never well informed about education, and I never had the choice. One minute I was in Belfast. The next minute I was in Hereford.'

The children did not feel able to complain; nor were signs of obvious unhappiness picked up. Like non-disabled children, some did find escape routes:

> 'When I didn't want to go to school I just went out and told the bus driver that I was going to the dentist and then I went back and told my Mum and Dad that the bus didn't come.'

Another respondent mentioned absconding from residential school and suggested it was quite common with the less disabled children. Cindy went to residential school at eleven-years-old on medical advice. She did not tell anyone she was unhappy, but knew it 'must have been obvious. I spent the first term crying myself to sleep every night'. This was dismissed as 'homesickness', a condition which the English seem to regard as character-building. This attitude prevents any meaningful efforts to ameliorate a child's unhappiness. Such failure to act on distress communicated by disabled children is found in many spheres, from alternative therapies to respite care, and reflects the unimportance of children's feelings against the needs and priorities of adults.

Special schools were also criticised for not preparing disabled children for the realities of the real world. Children were routinely misled about what they would face in life, and as such were sometimes ill prepared to meet it.

> 'It's OK they say, the world's going to be great with open arms and everybody loves you when in reality it's not true. You're going to leave and people are going to call you names, and you have to fight to get a job. No more covering in cotton wool.'

Mainstream schools, on the other hand, were criticised for not knowing what they were doing: for using disabled children as guinea pigs, being over-pleased with themselves for taking on a disabled child, or failing to recognise that disabled children were individuals who could not simply be processed through systems. Reactions to a disabled pupil were sometimes related more to standard formulae than an assessment of an individual's actual need. One respondent only needed help with science experiments, for which a lab technician could have been drafted in. Instead of this a full time assistant was employed for two years. This not only reflects poor resource management but such needless 'help' can be counter productive. Donald describes how his friends were put off because he always had a nurse nearby. Her constant presence was inhibiting to his friends. Another helper was 'a bit of a nightmare: she was possessive. At the time she was about 19 but I was only 11' . These examples are not evidence that classroom assistants are unnecessary, any more than criticisms of teaching methods imply there is no need for teachers. The issues that should be addressed are about matching the level of assistance to need, and giving assistants appropriate training so that they learn to facilitate, not control.

Praise for their education was rare, but shows that individuals can still make a difference. Billy greatly appreciated a teacher who persisted in trying to teach him maths: 'I failed it twice but on the third go I got it'.

A successful indicator of positive thinking was where teachers discovered and then concentrated efforts on developing things that the children could be successful at.

> 'There was one teacher, she was very supporting of me trying things. She said, give it a go. It doesn't matter if it doesn't work out. At least you'll have tried. It took the pressure off somehow.'

This meant taking the time to talk with students about what they wanted, and if necessary giving them the chance to try things out.

> 'There was this one teacher I got on with, but no-one else did for some reason, they thought he was a fuddy-duddy. He told me what was good. I know your parents do that, but for someone else to say this is really good. I appreciated that. It encouraged me.'

For some of the disabled students, the face value of their achievements was undermined by the belief of non-disabled students that far from being disadvantaged, they are over compensated and poor standards are overlooked. Successful young people can get into the 'equal opportunities trap' in which their success is attributed to sympathy for their condition.

'I won competitions for my designs. I did a couple of cover designs and I won twice running, but then I got "well, it's because of his hand". You know he's made an effort so they had to give it to me, just out of pity.'

'I once won this prize at school. I was about 13. I got a gift voucher in assembly at school, full of a thousand people, it was oh, like, they feel sorry for you.'

Choices and rights

'Choices and rights' is the theme song of the disability movement, but can seem like a distant ambition for disabled children whose experience is of not being in control. Deaf children are denied the right to effective communication.

'The teachers in (school for the deaf) were all hearing except two. If we signed in class we had to do lines as a punishment.'

Another means of exercising control was through physiotherapy, which was experienced as concentrating on the 'fault' to the exclusion of the child as a whole person, growing up with a range of needs. Children became alienated and rebellious and some simply opted out altogether.

'I hated physiotherapy, moving my limbs about. I couldn't see an end to it. I was put in splints to straighten my legs, like callipers. I stood up all day: it was like a table on my back. I had to eat my dinner like that. Somebody put me in it. I was strapped in it. I couldn't get out of it myself. I had no choice what-soever. I was stood up all day from the age of ten to eleven. It was painful and demoralising, and when I was twelve I rebelled and refused to have the callipers on. At thirteen the only way I could get control over my body was to get anorexia. I had got very overweight and they put me on a diet. So I stopped eating altogether. I went down from fifteen stone to six when I left school. They never picked up I was ill or unhappy, they were pleased I was losing weight. I was never put in for any exams or anything. I was the very bottom of the class. At fifteen I switched off. I was unruly. I nearly got expelled, because I told the geography teacher to fuck off and slapped her across the face. I was being denied my basic education.'

Some children were unhappy enough to rebel or to remove themselves from the system. Some actions sound like normal adolescent behaviour, such as 'messing about, smoking fags, getting drunk, being mouthy' and the reason may also be familiar: 'I was told I was stupid all my life and after a while you begin to believe it'.

The response to such 'challenging behaviour' for disabled children can be removal from mainstream education. In these cases it is perceived as a punishment.

Paths were chosen for disabled children because of tradition, from lack of imagination, mistakenly to protect them from disappointment or conversely to enforce normality. One student's mother made arrangements for him to attend after school activities such as 'swimming or Cubs every night', when he really wanted 'the odd night in'. Non compliance can prove as much a trap as following without question and Agnes found herself in a typical double bind. Her parents had whittled down her career options to becoming a physiotherapist or a piano tuner, both of which she was vigorously resisting because she needed to make up her own mind. She refused the opportunity to train as a physiotherapist not because she didn't want to do it, but because she was challenging what she saw as a destiny imposed because she was blind.

Disabled children's difficulties are made worse by the lack of control and of choice which they experience from an early age. As a result they can become over eager to please and lose the ability to think for themselves, or like Agnes, start to challenge everything: first as a matter of principle, and then simply out of habit.

> 'Everything I was told I could not do, I had to go for, whether or not as an activity it gave me any pleasure or not. It took me quite a while to realise what I was doing was just as dependent on others as was doing what I was told.'

Many children experience parental pressure, but the existence of a disability can provide a rationale for that control to be both deepened and extended for more years. Crucially, the disabled respondents *believed* that the pressure they experienced resulted from their disability. Attributing to disability problems which are part of many children's experiences as they grow up was a common finding of the research. It matters less whether or not this is true for any particular family, than what the child believes to be the case. Attributing all bad experiences to the existence of a physical impairment means a failure to realise how normal these experiences are.

One respondent describes a common experience of young people who are exploited by employers, but he attributes his own failure to be retained to his looks:

> 'I've worked for Y and Sons, got it and they let me go after my birthday. Well I got this letter and it said that due to the payroll budget they can't afford to keep me on. They took people on when they were busy and then they got rid of us. I didn't believe that. That was a load of rubbish. I had this feeling it was because of the way I looked because Y and Sons is very image conscious.'

Happily, the same young man had a positive experience with Mac-Donalds during a vacation job. What is sad about this is how simple his need actually was, and yet how rarely it was met in his life.

> 'I worked a bit at MacDonalds and they're very image conscious, and I was a bit concerned, but they were fine, they were fantastic about it you know. They spoke to me about my disability and that was the first time anyone has done that, which I appreciated.'

New social experiences such as moving to university are daunting for most people, but the need to mix with able-bodied people over-shadowed and complicated it for disabled students:

> 'You are talking to me about able-bodied people being afraid of disability, but I am afraid of meeting able-bodied people. I don't know how to talk to them. I was very scared when I first came here to the University.'

The origin of such beliefs probably lies in the reactions of others to the impairment, including the concentrated efforts to eradicate or disguise the fault. The isolation of disabled children from non-disabled con-temporaries may help feed the belief that *all* their experiences are dif-ferent, and militate against more balanced ways of dealing with them.

Medical interventions

Disabled children are categorised and labelled according to medical diagnoses, and thereafter can feel themselves to be dealt with less as individuals than as 'categories'.

> 'Children at my school were categorised by staff . . . put into boxes. You had to be partially sighted or you had to be blind. Partially sighted pupils had guide duties. My sight deteriorated, and I was moved from one box to another. This meant I lost friends, and I lost status, and although I could still find my way around, and I learned to use a guide cane, I was no longer allowed to guide visitors. My loss of sight meant loss of status automatically: no one assessed either my willingness nor my ability to continue to act as a guide'.

This status difference between 'blind' and 'partially sighted' was reported repeatedly by respondents and has been described earlier in relation to bullying. It may be that the differing privileges accruing to the different groups help to feed such jealousy if partially sighted children learn to regard themselves as better than those who are blind.

Physical faults are often 'corrected', presumably for medical reasons, at times when the young people may have other concerns and different priorities. Donald, for example, faced major surgery: 'rods down my back just before I went to secondary school'. He was already dealing with having to leave all his primary school friends behind, as the local High school was inaccessible.

Sometimes such surgery seemed a waste of time, and worse, the surgeons were less than honest:

> 'The arm was better when it was done but as time's gone on it's just gone back to how it was, because of the tissues there that are tight, they just pull back. What did annoy me to be honest was they never said this could happen at the beginning, it was oh it will be wonderful. Looking back if I knew then what I know now I would not have had the operation done. It messed up so many things at the time.'

Wayne talks of three operations he experienced to correct a deformed but functional hand, none of which were successful. Each operation to lengthen his arm involved breaking it and placing it in a large metal frame. The first coincided with his moving to comprehensive school, the second as he started his GCSEs, and the third over the period of his A-Levels, meaning he was unable to do practical-based subjects and had to drop design and technology. He had a talent for drawing, and later went on to undertake an MA in design. Zoe recalls more basic concerns: 'Pain, I couldn't be doing with it.'

It is strange how readily people deny that a disabled child experiences pain like any other. I have had frequent disturbing discussions on the issue with workers in child protection, who attribute inadequate or dilatory responses to the abuse of disabled children to a belief that disabled children do not feel things in the same way. Therefore the abuse is seen to matter less and may not be reported. This distorted perspective reflects our willingness as a society to conceptualise disabled children as less than fully human.

The 'children first' position has received considerable criticism from the disability movement, as implying that 'the reality of impairment – and the needs associated with it – can be denied', a statement I would not argue with (Kennedy 1996 p 130). However, the opposite is also true: the rights of a child can be denied if it is forgotten that disabled children experience pain, distress and embarrassment like any other child. In the case of alternative therapy, applying the principle that children should be treated as children first would end much real, if unintentional, abuse perpetrated in the crusade against disability.

The unwillingness or inability of the medical community to communicate sensitively with disabled children is reflected in the rejection of their help by some of the respondents. I found a high level of ignorance among the respondents about their own conditions, not only in terms of being unable to give it a name, but also about what it meant. Sandra dismissed her condition as 'one of those family things' while some of the others thought their parents might know but they had never asked. Since their conditions were fixed, most of the students were relatively uninterested in giving them names or knowing much about them, although they could see the importance of whether or not it was genetic:

'I'm not sure what you call it, but I know they told my Mum if she had another child it would have no arms, so I'm an only child.'

In one case not wanting to know was related to fear of dying:

'My friend, he'd got the same as me and he died when he was 14 because of it. Because I was a stubborn bugger when I was young I stopped going to see the doctors about what I had. I think I was trying to disassociate myself from my condition. But I don't know what my life expectancy is, I don't know what's going on. So I've got this little thing in the back of my head that I am going to live until I'm 60 or am I going to live until I'm 30?'

While diagnosis and prognosis may not have been important, the students were realistic about the difficulties which their impairments created, and resented the limitations placed on their childhood and their futures. Limitations which they accepted when they were young became harder to live with as they grew older. This was often expressed in relation to other children, but it reflects a personal struggle as well.

'If you hang around able-bodied people all the time I think you have a good chance of being bitter. Because I was, and I still am a bit. When I was in teenage years because I was in normal school I did get bitter because they were doing things, playing sports or something.'

All children have to learn to live with the fact that they cannot do and be everything that they might wish: accepting this disappointment is part of life. I was left wondering how well disabled children are helped to come to terms with real limitations, without the limitations being presented in a negative way, or stressed so strongly that they result in a constant battle to achieve for achievement's sake.

Images of disability

Disabled children learn lessons about their place in the world beyond their family and classrooms. They learn that they are seen by the majority as objects of pity, and can therefore be exploited. This exploitation is not simply by celebrities in events such as Telethons and Children-in-Need, but is deeply embedded in a culture where credit accrues to those seen to be helpful and charitable toward the less fortunate. Jason Awbery-Taylor reports:

'The local news-team for ITV Northwest, Granada Reports were featuring disabled youngsters in the area. They wanted to see how I got about; the school being so wheelchair unfriendly. I'd the timetable for my class altered so most of my lessons were downstairs, apart from computer studies and physics which were taught in their respective equipment labs upstairs. For these lessons I was carried upstairs by at first a sixth former and then by one of the teachers and when they got a bit of muscle by my friends. On the occasion of the televising the Headmaster just happened to be in the area.

We all found this highly amusing as he'd never carried me before, and as a matter of fact never did again.'

The head teacher exploited Jason to present himself as a concerned individual for the cameras, while those who were genuinely helpful on a day-to-day basis were ignored.

The other side of the coin ought to be positive images of disabled people. Jason Awbery-Taylor devoted some space to this in his auto-biography. He describes how having an article published in a careers magazine, and getting paid for it, was incredibly inspiring.

'From this point it became fairly clear what I should do – write. A thought kept running through my mind: "Jason Awbery-Taylor could be the new Stephen Hawking", but I seriously doubt reaching his pinnacle. Professor Hawking is a sufferer of Motor Neurone Disease – he fought the disease which will eventually kill him, to become the premier astro-physicist of our time. It's nice having a role model, anyway – he is, like me, a wheelchair-bound (and since a bout of pneumonia in the mid 80s took away his voice) Lightwriter user; so possibly you can see why I look up to him.'

Spurred by this, the students were asked if they had had any role models as children; who they wanted to be like when they grew up. Some of the male students cited football heroes, racing drivers and pop stars, among real people, and some also liked what they saw as the positive portrayal of disability and other physical difference in some television and film fiction.

The women, for reasons neither they nor I can wholly explain, all denied having any role models at all. It may relate to the greater emphasis in society on women's looks, or that the women were more realistic in their fantasies. Disabled women may find it harder to measure up to norms of physical attractiveness than men do. It might also explain the emphasis which the women students placed on finding a sexual partner who was non-disabled, since many women measure their social success, and their success as a woman, in terms of the status of their male partner. If all this seems a little old fashioned, it is worth remembering that a disabled young woman has grown up in a world which has transmitted the clear message that able-bodied is best, and made vigorous attempts to correct or disguise her impairments. Moreover, all women are bombarded with the message that they are responsible for, and can exercise control over, their bodies, from Government-driven health promotion to advertisements for beauty and health products.

Barron found in interviewing disabled young women that they did not think of their bodies positively, enforcing the view that growing up with a physical disability means thinking of bodies as 'not up to scratch' (Barron, 1997). The experience of physically disabled girls involved a great deal of physiotherapy aimed at correcting and making their bodies whole. Additionally, Barron points out that the media image of the ideal woman is not a wheelchair user. Attracting an able-bodied mate can act as a balance to these negative effects on personal self esteem, although placing such value on it reinforces the position of disabled partners as second best.

Several respondents cited the lack of disabled people on the television. They disliked the images they saw associating disability with passivity and old age. An old woman in a wheelchair on Coronation Street was thought unhelpful as she was someone who was disabled by age and had lived a 'normal life'.

> 'They should have somebody on Coronation Street with steam coming out of their ears because they can't get in the bar.'

Messages

Disabled children are in danger of being indoctrinated with a distorted view of life. The messages they receive are inconsistent, and are a mixture of truth, half-truth and lies which make it hard to separate out what is real. Some of the contradictory things disabled children are told or learn are as follows:

- The world is a nice place which will offer them charitable handouts if they ask nicely and respond gratefully. People who give are better than people who receive.

- The world is a nasty place where name calling and bullying are rife, but again, it is better to give than to receive!

- Teachers are bigger and more powerful than children, and may belittle, bully and physically abuse and get away with it.

- Schools and residential establishments are dangerous places.

- Special schools are safe places.

- Segregated education is 'special' and therefore good for them.

- They are stupid and will not achieve at school.

- They may as well opt out of schooling, as no-one expects them to get sound academic qualifications and there is no chance of finding employment.

- Their bodies are not nice, and they should expect to hide the way they look. They must be hidden or subjected to painful corrective procedures.

- Consultants have the answers, and operations to make them normal should take precedence over social or educational needs. It does not matter if these operations hurt, or need to be repeated, or are totally ineffective. They will add to the sum of scientific knowledge.

- There is every chance that any additional impairment or a medical condition will be overlooked or ignored, as the defining condition is often the only one that is seen. Having an impairment rules you out of normal medical examination and good basic health care.

- They do not need to be told the facts of life: about their conditions, about sex, or about relationships. They are especially not told that many of their difficult experiences growing up are not exclusive to disabled children.

- They are not worth as much as children who are unimpaired.

Discussion: a disability rights issue?

One question to explore is the extent to which the disadvantages identified in this chapter are applicable solely to disabled children and how far they reflect poor adult/child relationships in general. Are we looking at a fight to secure disability rights, or is it more than that?

Certainly most of the students in question blamed people's reactions to their disabling conditions as being at the root of their problems; they may well be right, but many non-disabled children are disappointed by their education, dislike being sent away from home, feel burdened by the vicarious hopes of their parents and rebel in their own way. Both disabled and non-disabled children are sexually abused, but it is often only in encountering other non-disabled survivors that some can begin to appreciate that there are common feelings about being abused which can be shared, whatever the reason for the abuse.

Both disabled and non-disabled children are abused within the care system, and can find themselves regarded as the problem, rather than the system. In his address to the North Wales Enquiry into child abuse in residential homes in Clwyd and Gwynedd, Gerard Elias QC notes that 'if the child reacted adversely within the care system, the child rather than the system appears to have been regarded as the problem' (*Guardian*, 17th March 1998).

The physical separation of disabled from non-disabled children makes it harder for them to check out these kinds of feelings and beliefs. In assuming their experiences are unique, the students were denying themselves the opportunities to share feelings with non-disabled young people and were thus reinforcing their own sense of difference. As such they were depriving themselves of a potential source of support and a way of belonging. This is doubly ironic, given the expressed wishes of most of the respondents to have friendships with both disabled and non-disabled people. They were also losing an opportunity to campaign on issues which concern all children, such as bullying in schools.

The author of the Cleveland Enquiry felt the need to note in her report what may seem obvious to many: that 'children are people, and not objects of concern' (Secretary of State for Social Services, 1988, p 25). It is not only disabled children, it seems, who find themselves objectified. This is not a society which naturally respects or listens to children. Susie Orbach writes of a culture of child hating in which children are divided into the innocent and the bad, and incidentally that this tendency to demonise or deify is also reflected in our dealings with teachers, mothers, fathers and social workers (Orbach 1997). Child hating may be an extreme way of expressing it but there is ample evidence that this is far from being a society which is child-centred, although some families may be. The court system in England and Wales is notoriously unfriendly toward children. The existence of league tables in schools places all children in danger of becoming commodities, of more or less value according to their ability to perform: it is an ethos in which children as individuals can easily get lost.

Alice's experiences growing up in the care system illustrate some poor childcare practices. There is insufficient data to reach any conclusion on whether her disability made social workers less mindful of her needs, but it is usually the case that social workers have fewer options where a child has an impairment. Alice went to school, lived with foster parents and then in residential care a long way from her natural mother. Her own lack of religious beliefs was ignored by a school which imposed a Catholic regime, while in her foster home she was raised strictly in line with the puritanical beliefs of her foster mother. The social worker responsible for monitoring her welfare was from the distant funding authority, rather than being a locally-based advocate. She was separated from her brother despite the fact that they were taken into care at the same time. Contact with their mother was minimal despite her expressed wish to maintain the link. All this flies in the face of knowledge that children require permanency, a sense of belonging and confidence in their own identity. It reinforces messages in the Utting Report that children in care should have advocates and independent visitors (Utting, 1997).

Understanding that some experiences are universal does not alter the fact that having an impairment means that a child can be discriminated against purely on the grounds of physical difference. This structural oppression will continue to undermine individual attempts and wishes to include and to be included.

Changing oppressive systems is a collective challenge. The respondents' relationship with the disability movement was interesting. None of the students conceptualised themselves as participants. Their comments represented a range of perspectives, from clear admiration for active protest to suggesting disabled people needed advocates.

'A disabled march last summer in London were chaining themselves to buses and I was saying YES. They were cutting them loose with bolt cutters. That was disabled people protesting, chaining themselves to buses and everything. That's what you need, because they are not going to give *them* anything.'

'*They* need someone to stick up for them. I always wanted to be a social worker: the guys were always dead easy to talk to. I think I could do a job like that. I can see what's not right and someone has to say something. Maybe it's me.'

Both these quotations carry a secondary message, which is that the students did not identify with the disabled people they were describing. Had they done so, the *them* and *they* italicised above would have been *we* and *us*.

Most respondents, in fact, did not identify as disabled, while some saw it as a negative label:

'I think of myself as a person. I don't like to think of myself as disabled.'

'I am disabled for the purposes of the University. It gives me longer in the exams and things. But its not a word I like using.'

This is interesting, since for many sections of society 'disabled' has become a symbol of struggle as an oppressed minority, and thus a group conveying a status to be proud to belong to. There have been arguments, for example, as to whether fat people should qualify (Cooper, 1997).

Tom Shakespeare interprets this denial of an identity as a disabled person as a phase disabled young people may need to go through if they are to be successful (personal communication, 1997). This may also explain the preference the respondents expressed for non-disabled partners. It is also interesting to note that high profile disabled people such as MPs are not necessarily advocates for others.

The students themselves did not, by and large, see their lives as struggles against their impairment. Many were surprisingly ignorant of and fairly uninterested in their medical conditions. Nonetheless they explained many of their negative experiences in relation to their disability. It was other people, physiotherapists and medical staff, who engaged in efforts to physically change children's bodies or appearances, often with painful consequences. The children saw life more as a struggle against institutions, systems and attitudes which created difficulties for them, because of the fact that they had a disability, or what the disability movement would term an 'impairment'. This was not their language, although their characteristic of attributing disablement to outside forces meant they had come to think in terms of a social model without having read about it, and with one exception without being able to give it a name.

Only one of the respondents was conscious of being exposed to disability rights literature or activism. They did not use words like 'rights', 'control', 'choice' or 'respect'. Their ambitions took the form of wishing to belong, to be valued, to mix with able-bodied people as well as in a disabled world, and to be understood. This was expressed in terms such as 'fighting' and 'making people listen'. A recurrent theme was not wishing to be dismissed as 'stupid', and it was salutary on analysing the interview transcriptions to note how frequently that word appeared. There was considerable bitterness and anger, directed at schools in particular, and at some individuals from all professions. All too often it was directed inwards against themselves.

In highlighting the kind of evidence presented in this chapter, there is a danger of perpetuating the picture of the pitiful disabled child which I was hoping to avoid when I embarked on this project. Disabled children are widely conceptualised as helpless because of the inherent difficulties of their physical impairment. Switching from a medical to a social model may only change the explanation for the disablement, so that the disabled child is still pictured as pitiful, but because of the sheer weight of external barriers to be overcome.

> 'Where the crippled child was portrayed as impotent in the face of deistic or biological fatalism, so the "disabled" child may appear impotent in the face of disabling barriers and structural oppression' (Priestley, 1998a, p 212).

To redress this impression, we need also to remember the resources disabled children themselves reveal in 'fighting back', even though for some the traits of rebellious adolescence became unhealthy and turned inwards. The resistance, resourcefulness and anger that they demonstrate as individuals should leave us optimistic that they may employ equal strength of purpose collectively in the future, and can make their contributions to the civil rights movement.

Ways forward

The respondents describe a disabling childhood, in which adult reaction to the existence of a physical impairment multiplies and exaggerates any inherent disadvantage in the impairment itself. Adults generally, and specifically some of those adults who are paid to care or to educate, are actively and *needlessly* making things worse.

At an individual level this can be addressed by recognising and reversing unhelpful behaviours. Dealing with the massive damage already visited on whole generations is clearly more complex, but this daunting task should not deter us from addressing some of the very straightforward lessons about how we treat children. The respondents proposed a variety of ways forward, some involving suggestions for disabled children's own activities, such as 'fighting tooth and nail' or, more constructively, that a deaf child get involved in the deaf community through Friends of Deaf Children (FDC). Others took the form of prescriptions for society at large, such as to stop looking at disabled people as objects of pity: 'The worse thing you can have is pity. People can't handle pity.'

The inevitable conclusion is that many children with impairments experience a great deal of avoidable disadvantage. This is not to deny the very real inconvenience, discomfort, pain and frustration that the impairment itself may cause, but to suggest that changes in the ways in which adults behave toward children with impairments can make a very real difference to their life chances and to their mental health. Children reporting to the Utting enquiry suggested that the kind of staff who would be helpful would have a good sense of humour, a good attitude towards children, try to understand them, and not shout (Utting, 1997, p 84). This seems a reasonable start.

What disabled young people are asking for from adults can be summarised as follows, giving an indication of the kind of workers children want. This list is derived from the students in the survey, with additional material from children interviewed by Butler (1998).

Young people want adults who

- stick up for them
- see them as individuals
- have a sense of humour
- are good listeners
- are not embarrassed by their disability
- will talk to them about being disabled
- talk about their abilities, rather than make assumptions about what they can or cannot do
- support and encourage achievements
- do not take control away
- do not impose religious or ideological beliefs
- help them develop social and relationship skills
- help them to meet other children, both disabled and non-disabled
- do not trivialise their concerns
- are honest and straightforward
- make them feel 'safe' in the sense of being trustworthy
- do not gossip about them
- do not smother them
- notice when they are unhappy
- do not act on information without consulting them
- do not pity, humiliate or abuse them
- don't make promises they can't keep.

Summary and conclusion

This chapter has provided illustrative data for a number of themes which will be returned to throughout the book, and to which responses from various service providers would be appropriate. The key areas, all of which illustrate disabling processes, are as follows:

- attitudes toward children who have impairments
- the undervaluing of disabled children

- internalised oppression/low self esteem
- structural abuse: belittlement, bullying, dehumanising
- unhelpful professionals
- institutional abuse in schools and residential establishments
- lack of positive role models.

These are interwoven themes. What emerges is a picture of childhood during which there is a steady negative stream of experiences which have cumulative effects. The overall result is that children who have physical impairments may grow up with lower self esteem, with lower expectations, a perverted desire either to please, or to rebel, and with an enhanced vulnerability to being abused. These results are not related to single incidents as much as to a prolonged experience of negativity and belittlement. There is an abusive trail from belittlement such as name calling, through more overt bullying, to physical and sexual assault. Coupled with the poor response of service providers to the needs of disabled children, this adds up to a depressing scenario in which adults, including those paid to care, may actually be *making things worse*.

Changing service provision involves a great deal more than reviewing existing procedures to make them more inclusive. We need to recognise the ways in which disabled children are socially and educationally disadvantaged, and be willing to challenge this; professionals in health, education and social welfare need to accept responsibility for their wellbeing, equality of opportunity and self esteem.

Chapter 2

Building Disadvantage

'The National Health service was founded on the principle that good quality health services should be available to all. Unfortunately, despite a great deal of progress, some groups and individuals are not getting a fair deal.'

Paul Boateng, Parliamentary Under Secretary for Health, in the Foreword to the NHS Executive Report, Signposts for Success (1998)

'It is not sufficient to consider services for the elderly, people with disabilities, or children at risk, without considering the kind of society and structures that create vulnerable groups within it.'

(Ann James, 1994, p 16)

'Oppression is your belief that you are better than I am, and mine that you might be right.'

(Laura Middleton, 1996, p ix)

'We all experience oppression as a result of the denial of our reality.'

(Jenny Morris, 1991, p 91)

Introduction

In what was described as a breakthrough in genetic engineering in May 1997, it became possible to detect the possibility of deafness in an unborn child. 'The discovery' concluded the report 'will allow parents to make preparations for their unborn baby *such as extra childcare and special schooling*' (my emphasis) (*Guardian*, 10th February 1998).

The illogical leap from learning a child may be deaf to making preparations for extra childcare and special schooling reflects the way we think as a society of disabled children as dependent and in need of special treatment. The counter argument that deaf children are only disadvantaged by this kind of attitude and the discrimination which follows as a result is neither widely heard nor accepted. Heaton, who is profoundly deaf, describes his own childhood as a constant battle with the priorities of the hearing world (Heaton 1998).

At its most basic a disabling system is constructed by how we think. For example, if people cannot understand someone who is speaking Japanese, they will tend to think this is their responsibility or because of a lack of education, but they do not usually blame the Japanese speaker. Japanese is socially constructed as exotic, foreign and part of the richness of humanity. Yet if someone cannot communicate with a deaf child, the chances are this will be attributed to the child's short-comings. We have learned that a deaf child cannot communicate with hearing people because of *their* disability. Unlike a Japanese child, a deaf child is socially constructed not as different but as defective. And yet this exclusion could be one of the easier ones to tackle.

One of the Preston students had the obvious answer:

'If I had a magic wand I would want all hearing people to sign a little bit. It should be part of the National Curriculum.'

The reasons for the persistence of disabling systems are discussed at the end of this chapter.

The political lead

Over the past 20 years the European Commission has published a number of resolutions and communications on disability which have included some reference to children, and these were brought together as guidelines in 1996 (European Commission 1995; 1996a, b, c). There has been a shift during that time toward a rights-based perspective which reflects that of the United Nations. The UN has issued a series of resolutions since the 1975 Declaration of Rights of Disabled people, which affirm the right of disabled people to equal rights and respon-sibilities within society. These do not have the status of law in any state, but imply a moral commitment for those countries who are signed up.

The European Commissioners are basing their work on the broad principles of equal opportunity and of challenging social exclusion.

'The historical policy response to disability has been largely one of social compensation through charity, separate provision outside the mainstream of society and the development of specialist caring services. However needed and well intentioned, these policy responses have arguably compounded the problem of exclusion and under participa-tion' (European Commission, 1996b, p 7).

Most of the work of the Commission relates to adults and is centred on their concerns. This 1996 communication recognises that some young people have problems in accessing mainstream education; however, unlike many of their other concerns, this is not translated into an implementation strategy. The 'concrete actions' outlined in the above document say nothing about schooling, nor do they address any inequality issues for children in terms of social welfare or health (p 4).

This is despite clear evidence, which will be illustrated later in this chapter, that children are subject to discrimination in many more areas than education.

This represents a fairly weak response to the needs of disabled children. This lack of any strong lead was also evident in the contradictory advice in the HELIOS II guide to good practice (European Commission 1996c). This Guidance was published after seven years of two programmes designed to promote social integration and equal opportunities: HELIOS I (1988–92) and HELIOS II (1993–96).The resulting Guide outlines eleven principles and eleven key aspects of good practice for education, which include the statement that:

> 'Everyone should have an equal opportunity to receive an adequate and appropriate education. The aims of education are the same for all learners.'

> (p 34)

And, more clearly:

> 'High quality mainstream education is an entitlement for all.'

> (p 34)

These principles are followed by eleven key aspects, the tenth of which declares, in direct contradiction of the Principle above, that special schools should continue to provide an alternative (p 44).

> 'In those cases where mainstream schools are unable to provide an appropriate education for a pupil, special schools should continue to offer a valuable alternative.'

> (p 44)

The HELIOS Guide also cites examples of good practice. However, schemes or organisations only need to illustrate 'one or more of the principles of good practice' to be included in the list (p 12). In spite of this low quality threshold, HELIOS II only cites seven examples of good practice in integrated education from across the European Union, one of which only had a single disabled pupil. Not surprisingly, the Guide has attracted criticism for inconsistency and lack of focused activity (European Commission, 1996c).

Answering the criticisms of the evaluator, the Commission declared that the HELIOS Programme,

> 'while very ambitious, is limited to the exchange of experience and information. It is not intended to make good any shortcomings in policies for which the Member States have sole responsibility.'

The European Commission further undermines its credibility by a declaration on the back cover that the Guide does not 'necessarily reflect the official views of the European Commission'.

All this may well leave the reader with the impression that the Commission has spent a great deal of time wasting it. Nonetheless, one possibly positive result of their actions is the language and concept of social exclusion, adopted by the Labour Government in the UK towards the end of 1997 when it set up its social exclusion unit.

Its key aims are:

- to improve understanding of the key characteristics of social exclusion, and the impact of Government policies;
- to promote solutions by encouraging co-operation, disseminating good practice and making recommendations for change in policies and delivery mechanisms.

The first phase, up to July 1998, concentrates on truancy and school exclusions. In February 1998 I wrote to the Unit asking about their plans for disabled children (see Appendix 2), and received the following reply, which I quote in full:

'Thank you for your letter dated 26 February.
We realise services for disabled children are very important, although not focusing on that specifically at present.
I enclose a leaflet about the Unit's work.'

The possible reasons why disabled children are not given a higher priority by the Social Exclusion Unit are considered later in this chapter. Here it is sufficient to note the neglect by central Government of a group so clearly disadvantaged. Taking the European Commission and the British Government together, the most positive thing that can be concluded is that they are consistent in their approach: neither are taking vigorous steps to end discrimination against disabled children.

There are two more positive official publications to note. One is the Utting Report which reviewed safeguards for children living away from home, and in doing so highlighted the situation for disabled children (Utting, 1997). There was nothing in the Report which was not already known to those campaigning for better protection services but it represents significant progress in official thinking. The Utting report is a recommendation to the Secretary of State for Health and at the time of writing, it is too early to judge the Government's response, although it is receiving widespread coverage.

Another potentially useful publication is the *Looking After Children* material prepared by the Dartington Social Research Unit (1995) to assess the wellbeing of children cared for by Local Authorities but which apply equally to those living at home. Since the authors probably did not have disabled children in mind when writing it, this list stops short of recognising issues such as discrimination, but it is a useful start. It provides a checklist by identifying seven dimensions essential to children's wellbeing:

- health
- education
- identity
- family and social relationships
- emotional and behavioural development
- self presentation
- self care skills

It follows that concentration on one aspect at the expense of others would be insufficient to ensure a child's wellbeing. A disabled child stands at particular risk of having medical needs take precedence over the wider aspects which contribute to a child's happiness.

SECTION I: Abnormalisation – The creation of special need

The rest of this chapter is divided into two main sections: this first section presents some illustrative evidence from the fields of health, education and social services of the ways in which services marginalise disabled children. The second section offers some explanations about why such discrimination persists.

Health care services

It is from the health sector that the interdisciplinary project is commonly managed. Thus disability has become a medical issue first and foremost. It is commonly defined, diagnosed, and conceptualised as tragic: a mother giving birth to a child with an obvious impairment will probably be moved to a side ward. Many disabling conditions are diagnosed at or before birth or in the first year of life, and are managed from hospital paediatric departments. A great deal of thought and care now goes into the task of 'breaking the news' but it still relies very much on the qualities of individual doctors. The tendency to conceptualise it as a single event rather than a process can lead to excessive shock for parents as well as putting pressure on doctors to make predictions which are beyond their current knowledge.

Conversations with social and healthcare professionals in the community reveal very similar concerns about the way health services are offered to disabled children and their families. The most frequently expressed were: the inadequacy and unfair distribution of resources; the low priority given to community as opposed to hospital care; the focus on child protection at the expense of family support; the difficulties operating across agency boundaries; unhelpful divisions in training and the inflexibility of means of delivery.

The healthcare of a disabled child is as likely to be overseen by a hospital consultant as by the family's general practitioner. There is a reciprocal tension whereby on the one hand hospital wards are reluctant to let go, as they lack confidence in their counterparts in the community to manage their patient adequately, and on the other the community-based staff feel undermined by hospital-based experts who fail to understand that a family home is not simply a side ward. Outreach from hospital has its place where there are serious medical problems, but many children who do not require acute medical intervention still remain under the wings of hospital departments.

This reflects a lack of understanding on the part of many hospital staff about what working in the community means. In simply extending the expertise of the ward staff, acute outreach services can disable by failing to appreciate how to work with whole families and with communities. Parents and members of the extended family, who could be supported and given confidence to care for their children, can become needlessly dependent on hospital-based experts who display limited confidence in their community-based counterparts. This was described to me by a health service manager as the 'Get 'em in' syndrome.

While medical specialisation may be justifiable for the development of expertise in particular conditions, and even to advise on their implications in a wider sphere, there is no medical reason why the day-to-day management of healthcare for a disabled child could not rest with the GP, as it does for other children. This is particularly true in an age when computerised 'health informatics' can provide ready access to patient information between institutions and medical personnel. Nor does being a medical specialist justify the behaviour of some consultants in overseeing the educational, social and psychological needs of the child. Oliver describes the predomination of the 'medical hegemony' in special education which contributes to disabled children growing up believing that they are ill and passively accepting sick roles (Oliver 1990, p 92). Perhaps it is the inability to cure, or even to explain in many cases, which leaves doctors with the need to take control even when their knowledge and skills are less appropriate than those of other members of the multidisciplinary team.

Heaton (1998) describes how intrusive the medical profession could be:

'After being diagnosed as deaf, I tried to get on with my childhood while being constantly interrupted to sit in a hospital chair straining for the slightest possible noises through massive ear-phone-muffled sounds which had no meaning and were not of the slightest interest.'

(p 12)

Disabled children and their parents are often managed through Child Development Centres which offer opportunities both for inter-disciplinary clinics and for parents to meet each other and share information and experiences. Although they are well regarded by many parents, this does not alter the fact that their very existence keeps disabled children away from normal clinical and pre-educational environments. Parents can easily become dependent on medical expertise, while the extended family may also believe themselves deskilled. Re-organising services between health centres and child development centres so that services used by all children would be under the same roof as those used only by some, would help ease the stigma for children while not depriving their parents of the support. The image of child development centres as only for problem children could be dispelled if they offered services for everyone, or if their work were subsumed into ordinary clinics.

Labelling some children as 'disabled' or 'special' sets them outside mainstream healthcare and disempowers both their parents, and the professional workers who may deal with them on a day to day basis. Outside the specialist system, nursery staff, teachers, paediatric and school nurses, social workers and play group leaders may never encounter a disabled child nor learn the essential lessons of acceptance. Disabled children grow up feeling different, stigmatised and afraid of meeting able-bodied children and adults.

Nor do disabled children receive the same quality of general healthcare from staff trained to focus attention on their impairment, and on the needs of their parents. As Chapter One illustrated, even obvious conditions like visual impairment, diabetes and a broken leg went unnoticed by staff who failed to see beyond the principal diagnosis. Disabled children are unlikely to be accorded the same priority for scarce or expensive resources. In Britain, Down's syndrome children are not considered for transplant surgery despite the fact that Down's children are the largest single identifiable group of children with chronic heart problems. Dr Radley-Smith at Harefield was unapologetic in an interview in the *Guardian*:

> 'It is not just Down's we are discriminating against. It is anybody with a disability. We take, when faced with a choice, the person who is the most *whole*, as it were.'

> (Toolis, 1996) (emphasis in the original)

Disability rights activists would argue reasonably that denying children medical care on the grounds of existing impairment, or according to their intellectual ability, is unacceptable. Such medical stances also beg questions about who decides who is 'whole' and what exactly constitutes a disability that bars a child from treatment.

The position of the disability rights activists is strengthened by Government-approved good practice as published by the NHS executive in the summer of 1998. *Signposts for Success* quotes the executive summary of HSG(92)42 (Appendix A) which gives people with learning disabilities the same rights of access to NHS services as anyone else.

It goes on to state that 'it is unacceptable to refuse or to offer inferior treatment to anyone on the grounds that he or she has a learning disability' (p 27). It is difficult to see how these principles could deny treatment to those with physical impairment. While Dr Radley-Smith justifies his position on clinical grounds, the ethical question is whether a disabled child has any less right to medical care than a non-disabled child.

Another ethical question is how far unproven interventions or treatments should be allowed. This takes us beyond the boundaries of scientific medicine into the realm of alternative treatments and therapies. Alternatives take root because the mainstream is deemed to have failed, and in the case of disabled children a considerable number of dubious therapies with no proven benefit have arisen. The concept of 'failure' in this context merits examination, since it implies that success was somehow possible and that it is worthwhile going elsewhere for different treatment. Disabled children cannot be 'cured' if they are not ill.

The alternative system has grown alongside scientific medicine, sometimes under the guise of education, sometimes religion. Conductive education developed in Hungary in the 1920s where the ability to walk was a condition of receiving education. Children were selected on the basis of their ability to learn this skill, and subjected to a highly structured intensive programme involving 'conductors' and specific equipment such as ladder back chairs. The mystique is deepened by the use of special terminology such as 'ortho functioning' and 'rhythmic intention'. Like many other therapies and methods, it has been spread by charismatic marketing. Conductive education has developed in various guises in such places as the United Kingdom, Australia, New Zealand, Hong Kong and Japan. Recent studies in both the UK and Australia indicate that the method has no advantages over traditional education (Barstow *et al.*, 1993; Bax, 1993; NHMRC, 1993). Alongside this lack of proven efficacy, after 70 years, has to be set the considerable expense and family disruption often involved in pursuing such methods. Organisations such as the Rehabilitation Centre in Philadelphia and the breakaway British Institute for Brain Injured Children (BIBIC) in Somerset use the fact of permanent disability to offer hope to parents, many of whom are consumed by guilt about their children, especially those who have been given little encouraging news by doctors.

There is no scientific basis for the efficacy of alternative treatments but those practising and profiting from such ventures have been allowed to continue on the grounds that they may at least offer comfort and support which conventional medicine seems unable to provide. Some physicians, such as Graves in Australia, have suggested more attention needs to be given to the opposing perspective of possible harmful effects (Graves, 1995). The harm seems all too obvious in some instances; some alternative treatments are drastic. If a social worker or policeman found a non-disabled toddler hanging upside down from her ankles in a doorframe, being spun around while she screamed and wet herself, they would undoubtedly start asking questions. Yet such indignities are visited with impunity on disabled children.

Suspended Inverted Rotation, one of the therapeutic programmes from Doman-Delacato, is claimed to increase children's spatial awareness and prevent the development of scoliosis, or curvature of the spine. It is an elaborate title for a procedure which means tying a child's feet together, hanging her upside down and spinning her around. Exponents of the process argue that as non-disabled children frequently hang upside down in the playground it is quite normal and must be good for them. Yet such play is only enjoyable so long as it is voluntary and controlled by the child. Children may indicate their fear or pain by crying, but the issue of consent is conveniently overridden when the activity is designated as 'therapy' not play. Another 'therapeutic' technique is the use of face masks which restrict the air supply and cause the child to breathe more deeply. This is supposed to increase lung capacity and thus improve the supply of oxygen to the brain.

The American Academy of Pediatricians issued a policy statement in 1982 to the effect that such treatment was unduly stressful and not proven to be beneficial. This has not prevented the spread of organisations offering such treatment to children across the world (AAP 1982). Graves concluded in a study based on a literature review on therapy methods that 'the claims for functional improvement could not be substantiated' (Graves 1995, p 24). In 1997 the British Royal College of Paediatrics and Child Health reached the conclusion that the intensive therapy programmes were 'uncertain, and that the discomfort to the children and the demands on the family may be considerable' (RCP 1997, foreword).

Patterning requires up to 5 helpers at a time, moving a child's limbs and head repetitively in an imitation of creeping and crawling. It is claimed to stimulate brain waves by teaching the damaged brain what to do. It is based on an idea established in Philadelphia in the 1950s that the central nervous system comprises evolutionary layers. The damaged nervous system must therefore be retaught movement sequentially, as fishes, amphibians, reptiles, mammals and humans (Fay, 1953). Scientific investigations into the techniques support the view that it is not effective (Sparrow & Ziegler, 1978; Cumming, 1988). Having limbs moved by others in such a way also carries the risk of pain, damage or dislocation.

Treatment under the Developmental Profile recommended by the BIBIC can last up to 6 hours a day. This not only ties up helpers for long periods, but uses up time which the child might make better use of in enjoyable play or social activity. A parent of a disabled child, who chairs BIBIC, writes that while it is impossible to guarantee results he prefers to throw everything 'into the fight' so he cannot be accused of not doing enough (Pennock, 1991). The difficulty with this view is twofold. First, all the efforts are aimed solely at correcting the impairment at the expense of broad-based development. Second, throwing everything into the fight against the disabling condition may actually cause harm to the child as a whole.

That these treatments go on despite objective evidence demands some kind of explanation. The Royal College of Paediatricians concluded that parents visit the Institute because of deficiencies in their local medical and therapeutic services. While this is undoubtedly part of the picture, an honest medical opinion is never going to offer a substitute for those needing to believe there is something more to be done. There are many stories of children being 'written off' by doctors who then go on to achieve well beyond expectations. Some of these children became University students and contributed to this book. This is testimony to the limitations of modern medicine: a characteristic we are reluctant to admit to, both as doctors or patients.

The ineffectiveness of the treatment is offset by the emotional support parents receive from the centre. Parents claim to feel more involved with their children's development than is usual with conventional medicine (RCP, 1997). While any progress can be attributed to the treatment, failure to progress can always be laid at the door of the condition which conventional medicine has already declared beyond its power or blamed on parents or children who have not tried hard enough. Given the complexity of brain injury, establishing controls for many scientific tests is difficult. Uncontrolled studies which report progress (Dickerson *et al.*, 1987) have been criticised since they cannot be certain about which changes are attributable to the passage of time (RCP, 1997).

The need to believe, or to demonstrate to others, that one is doing everything possible is an understandable reaction of many parents to having a disabled child (Pennock, 1991). Some devote considerable effort to correcting the fault in their child at whatever cost, and in doing so can inadvertently teach their child the lesson that they have to be physically 'normal' to be fully accepted. Wanting to do the best for one's children is entirely natural, but this wish may be intensified for parents of disabled children if they believe they contributed in some way to the impairment, and feel deeply guilty as a result. The disability may be attributed to having a child when they were older or had been advised against it, by smoking or substance abuse in pregnancy, or by physically abusing a baby or an unborn child. Such guilt may have a basis in reality or it may not; either way the efforts to make reparation relate more to the parents' need to forgive themselves than to any balanced evaluation of the child's needs.

Parents paying for unproven treatments are embracing hope rather than reason. The more exotic and expensive the illusion the better it may be in terms of meeting parents' need to 'do all they can'. The human body and brain are still sufficiently mysterious for almost any theory to sound convincing to a receptive ear. This would matter less if it did not carry serious implications for the child. Bleck has called for the search for a cure to be abandoned in favour of finding ways to support families:

> '...perhaps it is time to give up trying to "cure" the neurological defects by remedial methods, stop looking for positive studies, and get on with the task of helping children and their families.'

> (Bleck, 1987 p 212)

This unmet need of parents represents a failure in conventional services, which should be examined both for their sake and for the sake of the children who have to soak up so much unresolved pain on their behalf. Most staff and volunteers who deliver such treatments may genuinely believe they are doing good, but they may have suspended judgement about what is the right way to treat a child. They are able to do this because disabled children do not have the same status as non-disabled children. What seems to have developed is an attitude toward the use of unproven treatment for disabled children which maintains that it may as well be tried, it can't do any harm since they are already impaired. This ignores the very real pain, discomfort and indignity that children suffer as a result of these experiments. Children who are 'written off' by conventional medicine are sufficiently objectified to be regarded as subjects for experimental, high risk procedures which non-disabled children would not be exposed to.

Underpinning all this is the obsession of society with what constitutes normality. These treatments are not aimed at making the child happy, sociable, well or even comfortable but at moulding them towards *physical acceptability*. This is part of the continuum leading toward the myth of physical perfection which oppresses many people, but there is a cut-off point along that continuum; beyond it disabled children are labelled and separated from the majority in a way which adversely affects their life chances.

Inclusion is often confused with integration or assimilation. For disabled children the price of acceptance into mainstream life is that they conform to non-disabled definitions of normality. Parents are vulnerable to the marketing of alternative therapists who promise to 'normalise' their child. Children with Down's syndrome have had their eyes straightened to achieve a normal look. Walking, however ineffi-ciently, is usually promoted at the expense of using a wheelchair, even when this is more efficient. This is in spite of disadvantages such as present pain or future problems such as arthritis or dislocation. Chil-dren under such pressure learn to devalue their own bodies and often have to learn to like them later in life. If they fail to learn that lesson they leave themselves open to abuse.

One of the most graphic illustrations of an attempt to attain 'normality' was the effort to make thalidomide children look like able-bodied children by the manufacture of artificial arms and legs. This response reflected that used for people who have *lost* a limb, where artificial replacements are often the most appropriate response. This is quite a different situation from children who are born without limbs.

Thinking more creatively, Terry Wiles' parents manufactured a Supercar based on the principle of a fork-lift truck which was designed around his physique (Wallace & Robson 1975). Like many thalidomide children, Terry was born without either arms or legs. In working from his individual body, his parents recognised that his need for mobility was best met in a different way from most other children. A child born without legs has never learned mobility by walking, nor do children without arms have the usual means of saving themselves when they fall. In Terry's case, initial attempts to copy arms and legs artificially had left him effectively trapped in a heavy, monstrous and unsafe contraption.

These examples illustrate the need to think differently about what is appropriate for disabled children, and to be clear about what the real needs are, and where the assessment should begin. Mobility is important, but it does not necessarily have to be achieved through walking, any more than communication has to be through the spoken word.

Graves argues that powerful beliefs have grown up around many services for disabled children, such as 'more is better' and 'could do better if he tried' (Graves, 1995, p 26). These place responsibility on the parents and child and offer hopes for improvement which cannot be supported by the evidence. They lead in turn to constant demands for *more* services, and may draw attention away from exploring *different* solutions. Graves outlines goals for intervention drawing on the earlier work of Marfo and Kysela. This emphasises helping parents to overcome guilt, preventing undue disruption to normal child-parent interaction, and accessing community services (Graves, 1995, p 27; Marfo & Kysela, 1985). In this model the permanency of the disabling condition is accepted, and the aim of service provision is to work toward inclusion in the family and in the community. This would meet the concerns of the disabled students for a greater regard for their wider needs to be considered in assessing the case for medical intervention.

Education

In the UK, all children are entitled to free education until the age of 18 and it is compulsory until they are 16. This has not prevented the growth of special schools which take out of the system groups of pupils who are perceived as difficult to educate. Arguments for segregation, like those for residential respite, centre on worst-case scenarios. It is important to maintain a clear distinction between an argument which maintains, rightly or wrongly, that a child who is particularly difficult or disruptive should be temporarily separated from his peers, from an argument which holds that all children fitting certain categories, such as cerebral palsy, should be educated separately. That segregation may be right for some children some of the time is not a justification for its institutionalisation as a system of education. The only group of children for whom separate education may be appropriate are those whose first language is different from the majority, which includes deaf children, although this argument only makes sense if sign language is the teaching and learning medium employed. Many deaf children have been educated in segregated schools which insist on an oral tradition. The designation of deaf children as belonging to a linguistic minority is still a highly contentious area, especially since many of their parents have hearing.

The arguments for segregation centre both on the disabled and on the non-disabled child, both of which groups are claimed to suffer from being educated together. Such arguments focus on the disabled child as the locus of difficulty. They are deemed to be unable to cope, to be subject to undue bullying, to require an unfair amount of teacher time, or to be disruptive, or conversely to succeed better if educated in specialist facilities.

There are instances where disabled children do well in examinations in segregated schools, an example of which is the RNIB college described in Chapter Four. This educational achievement may be costly in social terms. The students in Chapter One describe the difficulties they had communicating with non-disabled contemporaries. Tomlinson and Colquhoun note that the receipt of any form of special education, even a special course in an integrated setting, may be unfavourably regarded by employers. They suggest that maintaining special education is a mechanism for legitimising non-employment (Tomlinson & Colquhoun, 1995, p 194) The new Labour administration elected in May 1997 is placing great emphasis on education and on implementing its 'welfare to work' policy. This work ethic includes disabled people, whose welfare benefits have been under threat as a result. The unemployment rate for disabled people is disproportionately high. Long term unemployment not only means lack of money but lower self esteem and exclusion from other activities such as leisure. Physical or intellectual impairment will prevent some people from being able to secure employment, as will prejudice, but disabled people will also be disadvantaged in the job market if they receive education which is of less high quality or prestige than their non-disabled contemporaries. It follows that if they wish to see more disabled people working, the Government could work towards improving the educational opportunities and standards for disabled children. Such expectations were increased both by the setting up of the Social Exclusion Unit in the Cabinet Office in January 1998, and by the fact that the Minister for Education at the time of writing, David Blunkett, is himself disabled. The first year of this administration has, however, failed to live up to these expectations.

As a group, disabled children are not conceptualised as future economically-contributing citizens, despite the fact that many disabled adults are successful and pay taxes as a consequence. Both they and the rest of society are conditioned to believe that disability equates with tragedy, burden and dependency. Instead of aspiring to normal educational expectations a disabled child is more likely to be cajoled to achieve in terms of eradicating their impairment as the price for acceptance. We make vigorous attempts to 'normalise' in terms of appearance and behaviour and set personal goals such as 'achieving maximum potential' or 'independence'. These are performance targets which no-one can seriously hope to achieve and are only likely to be set for individuals who are not taken seriously.

It is special education which has attracted the most criticism for failing its pupils. Special schools offer a poorer education than mainstream schools, rarely offer the normal range of examination subjects and inculcate social inferiority. Children are not sent to 'special' school because they are better than average but because they are judged unable to cope or are likely to be disruptive in normal school. The child rather than the school is seen to fall below standard.

Ford (1982) suggested society has little sympathy for those with disabling conditions, and many people remain ambivalent about the part disabled people can play in economic life. The goal for much special education has therefore been to achieve 'independence' or 'self sufficiency' rather than to prioritise educational or examination targets, so that disabled adults would not be dependent on State help. Expectations about progression up career ladders beyond achieving non-dependent status are rare for disabled children. Thus special education becomes a form of social control. Tomlinson (1982) argued that the aim of special education was to enable disabled children to fit unobtrusively into adult society, not to enable them to achieve educationally, or to secure employment. In this sense independence implies no more than achieving an economic balance with society, not making a contribution to it, and can therefore be defined as a low level ambition.

Attempts to help can further disadvantage. The student in Chapter One who felt constrained by his ever present adult assistant was by no means the only one. Over-intrusive adult helpers can work against the normal social processes which enable acceptance by other children. It is harder for a disabled child with a helper to misbehave, pass notes or play with their virtual pet (Priestley 1998a). Formal adult help from classroom assistants or social workers constrains the normal dynamics of peer friendship (Priestley 1998b). Hirst & Baldwin (1994) note that children in special schools are disadvantaged in terms of self-esteem and social relationships compared with those in the mainstream.

Heaton (1998) describes his shock on leaving a special school for deaf children to discover that the speech he had thought 'excellent' while there was incomprehensible to his fellow workers:

> 'I had to relearn how to deal with the world, and the first step was to throw my hearing aid in the bin.'

(p 12)

Teachers who respond differently to disabled children out of misplaced sympathy do not help either. The students in Chapter One described how their achievements were often dismissed as favouritism or as being judged according to different standards. Priestley found that disabled pupils are less likely to be disciplined. This cuts across children's sense of fair play and sets the disabled child apart, reinforcing messages of difference and special need. Disabled children can learn to use their disability as a reason not to produce work on time, or to standard (Priestley, 1998b).

While some parents recognise the disadvantages of special education, and strive to have their child admitted to mainstream school, there are still some who choose to continue to opt out. Given the major educational and social disadvantages of segregation this needs some explanation. One possible conclusion is that education and social status are not valued by parents as highly as the *perceived* advantages of segregation, such as safety, the availability of physiotherapy or nursing care, or a wish to shield their child from curious or thoughtless attention. However it may be that either such parents simply do not know enough, or that they do not have access to sound advice or support to enable them to take a long term view.

In a keynote address to an international conference on Special Education Michael Oliver asserted that special education has been

> 'an abject failure on whatever criteria are used to judge it . . . If we say that the purpose of such provision is to provide an equivalent education to that of non-disabled children, it has failed. If we say its purpose is to provide a basis for the full integration and participation into society of disabled children when they become adults, it has failed. If we say that its purpose is to provide a special form of education to meet the special needs of disabled children, again it has failed.'

(Oliver, 1994, p 67)

The problem is that none of these are the criteria against which special education *is* judged. Special education is evaluated less on its contribution to the needs of its pupils than on its contribution to the education system as a whole. It is not intended primarily to benefit those within it, but to protect the majority of children from the perceived disadvantages of being educated alongside pupils who would disrupt, hold them back, command too much teacher time, or are simply not considered pleasant to look at. In other words, special education is used to maintain 'disability-free zones' in mainstream education. This has official backing. The law in England and Wales gives Local Authorities a *Qualified Duty* to secure the education of children with special educational needs in ordinary schools unless there are specific reasons why not, namely:

• not meeting the child's special educational needs
• achieving efficient education for other children
• making efficient use of resources
  (Education Act 1993 Section 160, England and Wales).

In effect, this means that disabled children can only be educated alongside non-disabled children provided the latter are not likely to be disadvantaged in the process.

The law which has been introduced ostensibly to effect changes has been ineffective in making any fundamental difference to provision. It has been argued that any change which has occurred has been dependent on pressures exerted by interested individuals or pressure groups working for particular children (Stakes & Hornby, 1997). The most important advocates for disabled children have usually been their parents. This has not been an easy role to fill. Parents are not always welcomed as partners by teachers despite considerable evidence that children's education benefits from such involvement (Stakes & Hornby 1997). The 1981 Education Act established the framework for the parent as advocate, but did not necessarily equip them for the task. Organisations such as the Children's Legal Centre and the Centre for Studies on Integration in Education (now 'Inclusive' Education) have provided information and legal advice, but the vast majority of parents are reliant on local education authority staff. Nor is acting as advocate for one's own child without its pitfalls, as the child grows up and develops opinions of his or her own. The evidence from the students interviewed is that they did not necessarily have the same priorities for their education as their parents. The perspective of consumers of the education system deserves to be taken seriously. This applies to any young person, but it is particularly important for those who are disabled since, in most families, the disability is an experience their parents will not share.

This difference in perspective also applies to professionals. Heaton (1998) noted that he comes across 'significant numbers of (deaf) students who report that the system has failed to accept that their priorities are different from those professionals who have so much power over them' (p 12). He argues for a forum in which to 'add to' the professionals' understanding of deaf children's lives.

The 1981 Education Act was criticised by Neil Kinnock as being akin to using Brighton Pier as the route to getting to France: 'OK as far as it went'. It went further than previous legislation in focusing attention on the needs of disabled children, and provided for the assessment of educational need on an individual basis rather than by category, handicap or diagnosis. The 1993 Education Act and Code of Practice sought to strengthen this, although the latter carried no mandatory duties and is considered over-bureaucratic by the Special Needs Co-ordinators appointed to implement it (Dyson & Gains, 1995; Stakes, 1996). It has also been criticised for following a medical model including the key role in assessment played by doctors, undue emphasis on 'diagnosis' and its consequent remedial action, and the focus on the shortcomings of the individual child (Stakes & Hornby, 1997). Humphreys & Gordon (1992) suggested that children with special educational needs were labelled and categorised as unworthy and incapable, both academically and socially, which contributed to their feelings of low self esteem.

The Code's potential to improve provision has been hampered by inadequate funding, both for schools and for extra teacher-training. This was thought in many quarters to be an attempt by Government to reduce spending on special educational needs (Hornby, 1995). Schools have changed the threshold levels at which pupils receive extra help. The result of reducing the number of eligible pupils is that parents who require help are pressured into emphasising problems in order to secure it. This involves similar dynamics to rationing in social services, as will be described later in this chapter.

There is little evidence of any strong political will from Government to produce the resources to make this legislation work. Leaving teachers to solve problems at classroom level has resulted in large scale dissatisfaction and an unwillingness as a profession to pursue integration (NUT, 1995). Suggestions about ending special education produce statements about disrupted classes, challenging behaviour and the lack of nursing provision. For example Nigel de Gruchy, the General Secretary of the National Association of Schoolmasters, told their annual conference in 1996 that 'The closure of special schools has wreaked havoc in the education system.'

Special education is marketed to parents as a safe option for their disabled child, who would otherwise be vulnerable in the hurley-burley of mainstream education. This is a powerful argument, in which the long term view (that only in that hurley-burley can children learn to live with each other) is easily lost in the natural wish to protect them from being hurt or from feeling marginalised.

Bullying in schools is a serious concern. In a letter to the *Guardian*, Jacqueline Flanaghan writes of her concerns about her 'statemented child' being educated in a mainstream school:

> 'As a parent of a statemented child, I am disturbed by the assumption that these children are better served in mainstream secondary schools. Many are subjected to severe bullying ... they feel different from their classmates when they are taken out of class to be taught separately in special needs units.'

(*Guardian*, 28th October 1997)

This highlights the very real lack of confidence felt by parents in sending their children to mainstream schools. Sadly, special schools are not the haven from bullying that she implies, nor are children with special educational needs necessarily nice to each other. The evidence is that they bully other children and establish pecking orders just as children do in other schools. Many of the respondents in the research study in Chapter one told of being bullied, or of engaging in it.

The problem is that the educational system is not organised to provide a rounded education, either for disabled or for non-disabled children. It does not prioritise the need for children to learn to live with, respect or care for each other. Success is not measured in terms of building confidence, teaching children to make friends or even to learn how to play with each other but rather in terms of examinations passed. Its core business is to work toward academic or vocational qualifications to serve the labour market, not to teach social skills. In that vacuum children make their own rules, reflecting and aping the behaviour they see around them in the adult world where bullying is endemic.

While in the broad sense disabled children are no different, in that they are both victims and perpetrators of bullying, there are two crucial factors to bear in mind where they are concerned. First, their impairment is likely to be the focus for bullying. They may well have already learned that this is a 'bad' aspect of their body. It may have been surgically altered, or attracted corrective attention from therapists. It may cause pain, discomfort or prevent participation in sport or games. This all makes it doubly hard to ignore taunts. Oppression is not simply the power which one group exercises over another: it is also how the targeted group is made to feel about themselves as a result (Middleton 1996). The disabled child is likely to internalise the oppression, and agree with his tormentor that he is worth less than they are.

The second factor is that unlike racial bullying, the chances are that the child's parents do not share the targeted characteristic and can neither empathise nor speak to their child from personal experience of dealing with it. Many parents of disabled children have to learn to deal with the problem at the same time as their child. Taunts may be unexpected, leaving parents no opportunity to prepare their children for them. They may also suffer the child's accusation that they 'don't know how it feels'. Small wonder that many opt for the 'safety' of special education and the companionship of other parents with similar children.

There is another key factor to consider: the case against special education will only be won when mainstream education offers a better alternative. At the moment it is all too often non-inclusive in any real sense. Jacqueline Flanaghan thought teachers were often left to 'muddle through'. In some schools lack of support for inexperienced staff is a serious problem, which mirrors that of parents left to manage on their own at home. Some schools fulfil their moral obligation by taking on a single disabled child. Yet an isolated disabled child is always at risk of becoming the school project. As such he or she will carry the burden of representing disabled children as a whole, as well as educating the non-disabled school about them. Like Jason Awbery-Taylor in Chapter one, she may even find herself being photographed with the headmaster!

Many mainstream schools clearly have yet to get it right, and many parents do not trust their disabled children to them. Yet there are increasing numbers who recognise that special simply means second best. Where parents do want their children to attend mainstream schools, they often face the objections of the local education authority or of the head teachers, and yet their case is undeniably just. The simplest and most convincing case I have read was that of Mrs Crane, who lost a three year fight with Lancashire Education Authority to send her 14 year old son to the same school as his sister and his friends:

> 'Niki cannot understand why he cannot go to the comprehensive. He has done nothing wrong.'
>
> (*Guardian*, 28th October 1995)

His father added the indisputable point that schools were not comprehensive if they chose pupils on the basis of ability or disability. Despite these arguments, Mr Justice Popplewell ruled that parental choice could be over-ridden since 'the education of other children *could* be disrupted if he attended and that the expense of meeting his special needs there would not be cost effective' (my emphasis).

More recently a mother in Belfast received a twelve-month discharge by magistrates in Belfast for 'wilful non-attendance' for refusing to allow her son to attend a special school.

> 'The government seem to believe in inclusion, but this is being denied my son. I've never wanted to see him separated from the rest of the community. If he goes to a special school it will be much harder for him to interact with wider society when he finishes his education.'
>
> (*Independent on Sunday*, 12th April 1984)

Parents, teachers and politicians are all having their say in the educational debate. Children's voices are conspicuous by their absence. The young people in Chapter one set out their own priorities in terms of education very clearly. They felt deprived by low expectations of them, and by the lack of opportunity in schools. They felt written off and patronised. Medical interventions deprived them of education at crucial stages, while intrusive classroom assistants could set them apart from their friends. They wanted to be pushed, to discover their abilities, and to succeed. They valued friendships and wanted to be able to retain them without the barriers created by distance, transport and changes of school. They wanted to have a sense of control over their bodies and their lives. Most of all they wanted to like themselves.

None of these seem unreasonable aspirations. Any attempt to reform the educational system has to take the children's needs and wishes into account as well as the views and opinions of parents and teachers, if it is to educate the next generation in a fairer way than the last. However, special education will not be phased out simply because those directly affected by it, or even those working within it, decide there is reason to reform. The parents and teachers of the non-disabled majority also need convincing that better education for disabled children will not be to the disadvantage of their children. As long as children are conceptually and administratively separated into distinct groups this destructive 'us-and-them' debate is likely to persist at the expense of more productive discussions about ways in which the educational system can be improved to benefit and include all children.

Welfare services

Discrimination in welfare has attracted far less controversy than in education or healthcare, but it is equally unacceptable. This section illustrates such disadvantage using examples from respite care and child protection services, and describes ways in which parents interact with welfare providers. It then discusses the independent/statutory divide which affects both educational and welfare provision.

Respite care

For most families with a disabled child, respite away from home remains the main plank of welfare provision, and is still used in circumstances that would not be thought acceptable for non-disabled children of the same age. All parents need breaks from their children; the extent of their need depends on a range of factors, including the abilities of the parents, the support available to them, their work and family commitments and the character of the child or children in question. Yet although this need is quite normal, respite services for the parents of disabled children are typically managed separately from those for non-disabled children. Foster carers can refuse to take a disabled child without criticism even if there are no specific medical dangers. In some authorities foster care services for disabled children are contracted out to the independent sector. Family link workers or family aides provided by social services frequently do not include either recruitment of carers for disabled children, nor offer their carers training about disability issues. Services are provided instead through separate, specialist disability teams.

While in most authorities there is a spectrum of care possibilities, from family group homes and family-based care to help in the child's own home, disabled children are more likely than non-disabled children of the same age to be provided for away from home, in paediatric wards or in building-based specialist respite care homes.

Beresford and her colleagues, looking at service evaluation in the UK, make the very deliberate choice to call their book 'what works for families with a disabled child' rather than 'what works for disabled children', on the grounds that the evidence for the latter is not available:

> 'we have often failed to even seek to listen to what disabled children and young people have to say. The minority status ascribed by society to children and disability has doubly disadvantaged the disabled child in terms of being consulted and involved in research and development work.'
>
> (Beresford *et al.*, 1996)

As a consequence their criteria for what works are family centred, and are particularly focused on adult carers. They cover such areas as information, material resources, breaks from care, domestic help, skills and social support. By and large these areas will not address the concerns that the children outlined earlier in this book.

Research has concentrated on exploring how children adjust to such care, rather than on its appropriateness. It has confirmed that many young children dislike being away from home, and that their parents feel guilty and miss them (Robinson, 1987; Stalker, 1990; Stalker & Robinson, 1991). Children are sometimes sold the idea as a 'holiday' or an opportunity to make new friends, but it is rarely experienced as such. Research in Liverpool found that the randomness of respite, together with a changing staff rota, mean a slender likelihood of establishing relationships or making friends. On the contrary, children who used respite frequently experienced the loss of significant relationships and sense of place (Flynn *et al.*, 1994). This loss of relationships is of particular concern where the child comes from a minority community. Neither staff nor the other children in an away-from-home respite are likely to reflect the ethnicity of a minority group.

Being sent away from home to relieve pressure on one's family not only carries all the usual hazards such as homesickness, but also the stigma of being the burden (Middleton, 1996). Respite reinforces the status of the disabled child as a 'problem' for a family, rather than an individual with needs of her own. This essential conceptual difference enables service providers to ignore or over-ride the childcare and child protection practices that they would usually apply, and offer service according to different criteria. It is still the practice in some local authorities to remove pre-school age disabled children from home into special nurseries for respite care. When these babies show signs of distress or develop 'challenging behaviour' this is easily attributable to their disabling condition.

Recent thinking has recognised that such respite should be child-centred. The preferred term has changed to 'natural breaks' and plans include siblings. Adopting this approach would move services nearer to support in children's homes and communities and by their own families. Flynn proposes that if services could be recast so that they are family-centred and

> 'hinge on the importance of building enduring relationships with other children, foster families, home based respite carers, family friends, family aides and respite support workers, then the case for away from home units becomes weaker and in turn, the expectations of future support more person-centred.'

> (Flynn *et al.*, 1994, p 49)

As a starting point some consensus is needed that respite could make a positive contribution to the child *and* family; that childcare principles should be equally applicable to disabled and non-disabled children and that more flexibility in terms of services available is a desirable objective.

Child abuse

The following extract is from an anonymous letter sent by a student nurse about her placement to her university's student newspaper. Ominously, the editor introduced it as representing a common situation.

> 'My first placement, learning disabilities with children and I was determined to really make an effort. I wanted to be a valuable member of the team. So when I noticed that one child was not getting as much attention as all the others, I decided to really focus on this child. So I sang to him, I read stories to him, all day long I talked to him. No response, not a word, not an action, nothing to give me any indication that I was getting anywhere. So I asked the staff, who had happily let me get on with it, why I was not having an effect. It was only then that they told me that the child was blind and deaf. How they enjoyed watching me. Bastards.'

> (Anonymous, 1997)

This letter graphically illustrates how professional staff can so objectify and ignore the feelings and dignity of a disabled child that they are willing to make use of him as part of a humiliating induction process for a student. This begs all sort of questions not only about the attitudes of the staff concerned but also about the quality of education the student is receiving. Arguably a young person with a humane outlook is on the road to being conditioned not to offer help but to laugh at others.

Indulging in belittling and undignifying behaviour is the thin end of an abusive wedge which leads to serious abuse of cared for children. It is important for the future treatment of disabled children that this connection is recognised, and that the line around behaviour which is unacceptable is drawn early.

Physical or sexual abuse gives a feeling of power to someone who might otherwise feel powerless or who has problems with normal sexual or social relationships. A disabled child who is physically less able to defend herself, run away or identify her attacker is an attractive target, but is made all the more so if she believes that she is worth less than a non-disabled child, and puts less value on herself as a result. Disabled children inculcated with low self esteem are more vulnerable to the predations of adults offering 'love' than those who have grown up to respect themselves and their bodies.

Not only does respite away from home carry the kind of emotional and relationship disadvantages described above, it can also be physically dangerous. Research into child abuse indicates that care away from home is no safer for a disabled child than for any other child. Indeed, the sheer numbers of carers involved with such children may actually increase the level of risk (Westcott & Cross, 1995; Morris, 1996a). Children away from home not only lack the protection and support of family and friends, but their isolation from local communities sends messages to potential abusers that they are uncared for and unvalued and can be targeted with relative impunity.

Disabled children in residential accommodation or foster care are less likely to receive independent visitors than non-disabled children, although the situation is poor for all children in such care. Despite the requirement of the Children Act (England and Wales) 1989 that local authorities provide visitors for all children who have lost contact with their parents, only $\frac{2}{3}$ of local authorities operate independent visitor schemes reaching only four per cent of eligible children. This situation is even worse for disabled children, of whom only about one per cent of those eligible had allocated visitors, despite their popularity with those children who did receive them (Knight, 1998). The Utting report recommended the extension of the independent visitor scheme to all children who 'might benefit', a much wider category than those in care, but there is no evidence that this is being acted on (Utting 1997). Anecdotal evidence from social workers and nurses indicates that far from being on the decline, unsuitable placements for disabled children such as residential schools, hospices and hospital wards continue to be used, and private sector placements are on the increase. Such placements lack the same levels of safeguard either of assessment or of review normally provided under the Children Act for 'accommodated' children. Failing to protect children in the residential system is a serious problem made worse for disabled children both by the range of placements available and by the indifference to their situation shown by many inspection units in both social services departments and health authorities (Morris, 1996a). The Utting report acknowledged this omission and recommended the

Children Act be extended to include the inspection of residential special schools (Utting, 1997):

'They should be entitled to the same range of protective measures as other children whether they live in a residential home, foster care, spend 52 weeks a year in schools or spend substantial periods of time in hospitals or nursing homes'

(p 84)

'We believe there is scope to extend existing inspection and regulation in order to provide greater safeguards for disabled children in schools. Chapter 4 recommends the extension of Section 87 of the Children Act to all maintained and non-maintained special schools.'

(p 85)

The increased segregation in disabled children's services is threatening the fragile growth in awareness of the abuse of disabled children and the consequential changes in the child protection service (Kennedy, 1989, 1990; Kelly, 1992; Marchant & Page, 1992; Westcott, 1993; Westcott & Cross, 1995; Morris, 1996a; Middleton, 1996). Disability organisations tend not to consider child protection to be part of their remit. Workers in independent sector childcare organisations are largely shielded from child protection work. Nor is the NSPCC offering the lead it might do in this area. Despite NSPCC sponsorship for research and for the ABCD training resource pack (Westcott, 1993; NSPCC, 1993), the protection of disabled children is as much a separate enterprise for the organisation as a whole as it is for local authorities. This lack of direction from the national centre is proving frustrating for some of their regional staff, one of whom noted in a letter to me that the needs of disabled children were 'not particularly prominent' in the NSPCC's vision for the Millennium [personal communication, 1997). There is apparently little pressure from government to alter this state of affairs.

The Audit Commission (1994) and the Dartington Research report 'Messages from Research' (1995) raised concerns about the appropriate focus and direction of social work with children, especially those at risk of abuse. Yet neither the Department of Health, who commissioned the research, nor any of the universities who undertook it, saw fit to include disabled children in their work. The authors of the research were so unembarrassed by this omission they were even prepared to highlight it in the introduction to the report:

'It is the case that important groups, such as children with disabilities, those placed for adoption or those living in residential or specialist foster care, are not specifically dealt with. Similarly issues of race, gender and rights may not be as salient in the studies as *some readers* might wish' (my emphasis).

(Dartington Social Research Unit, 1995)

Those exacting readers might also have noted that not only do all the 'important groups' include disabled children, but that they all constitute groups of children at high risk of abuse.

Abusers feel safer attacking disabled children partly because of opportunity, but also because of their perceived or real helplessness and their inability to disclose. They may also be less likely to be believed. Disabled children who are abused may need extra help in understanding what has happened to them (Kennedy, 1990). This is a complicated issue. Many disabled children conceptualise themselves as 'burdens', and may believe that either they, or their parents, are somehow 'bad' or being punished for something. The disabled child who assumes she is being abused because she is disabled needs a great deal of help to sort out these dynamics, since it may be true that she was targeted because of her vulnerability as a disabled child.

That professionals need to develop a better understanding of these complexities is not an argument for separate services, but for the training of child protection workers to include the ways in which abuse may be experienced by disabled children. This approach means that the specific issues for disabled children are understood within a context of sound childcare principles and knowledge of child protection practices. Behaviours and service responses which would be considered unacceptable for non-disabled children are equally so when the child has a physical impairment.

The role of parents

Discrimination does not just affect disabled children, but also their parents. The Children Act 1989 had clear aspirations in terms of family support and the promotion of partnership, which have been difficult to realise. There have been a number of studies to explore this, but perhaps the Government's own view in the Children Act Report 1993 is the most convincing (DoH, 1994). This concluded that services had failed to move from a reactive, policing role, to a proactive, partnership approach with parents and carers. Certainly there is little evidence that parents of disabled children consider themselves to be in partnership with local authorities.

There has been a considerable amount of research into the needs of parents of disabled children, but the pressures on them to act in particular ways to secure resources are not always recognised. In order to secure what could be commonplace resources, they may have to present their children as especially difficult or demanding. This is part of the process of creating special need. It marginalises disabled children and uses their own parents as instruments of that marginalisation.

Research focusing on those caring for disabled children, usually mothers, consistently documents the isolation they feel and the lack of support available (for example Glendinning, 1983; Byrne & Cunningham, 1985; Sloper & Turner, 1992). Later work by Beresford (1994) has changed the focus from parents as victims to a more positive examination of their coping mechanisms, but such a shift in emphasis does not alter the underlying picture of parents receiving too little support from both statutory and voluntary services. Other researchers have noted adverse effects on finance (Baldwin, 1985) and on personal, especially marital relationships (Weale & Bradshaw, 1980; Hirst, 1991). Bamford and his colleagues analysed consumer satisfaction with services in cerebral palsy care, across the medical, educational and social care professions. Their findings indicated high levels of satisfaction with core medical help, some key paramedics and with teachers, but glaring deficiencies when the concept of care was broadened to include social, psychological and emotional needs (Bamford, *et al.*, 1997).

Research in 'Waterside' confirmed the finding of much of the earlier research (see Appendix 1). Parents' views were depressingly predictable: indeed such views have changed little in the last 15 years. They reflect confusion about service provision, ignorance of their children's legal (as opposed to moral) rights, a preference for proactive service provision, and the need for emotional as well as material support. This last was framed variously as a need for counselling, advice and someone to listen. There was little evidence that the Children Act (England and Wales) 1989, which could have facilitated improvements in all these areas, had made any discernible difference (Middleton, 1998c). This research also showed the lack of importance accorded by welfare services to the parents' needs.

'About three years ago I requested a social worker and I could not get one. Every time I phone up I can only get to talk to the duty officer and I said I am fed up with trying to explain all about my family to a stranger every time.'

(pp 243)

It also highlighted the need to fight: that parents have to make the running in a reactive service and that confidence is needed to ask for help, which means having a good reason. It was widely believed that social workers only responded if children were thought to be in danger: 'you have to batter your child to get their attention'.

If parents are to avoid the epithets of being non-coping, problematic, or abusive, some alternative explanation is needed. Instead of casting themselves as non-coping, parents learn to stress the abnormality of their burden. This is not difficult since disabled children clearly can make extra demands on parents. Nonetheless, it is a short step from there to exaggerating the child's level of impairment in order to maximise the service response. Parents, like any consumers, learn to frame their demands according to expected responses.

The message they seek to convey and to which social services will respond, is that they need help not because of inadequate parenting skills, but because their child is exceptionally difficult. In this way, the rationing practice of social services creates a scenario which casts the child in the role of family burden. Faced with the methods used by services who allocate according to their own definitions of need rather than the consumers', individuals seeking the best outcome must tailor their case accordingly. The six levels of assessment in the guidance to the NHS and Community Care Act 1990 range from simple to comprehensive and increase the problem for consumers by tying the status of the assessor with the original perceived need (see Fig. 2.1).

Assessment	Need	Staff
(1) simple	simple, defined	reception or admin
(2) limited	limited, defined, low risk	vocationally qualified
(3) multiple	range or limited, defined, low risk	vocationally qualified
(4) specialist		
(a) simple	defined, specialist, low risk	specialist ancillary
(b) complex	ill-defined, complex, high risk	specialist professional
(5) complex	ill-defined, interrelated, complex, volatile, high risk	professionally qualified
(6) comprehensive	ill-defined, multiple, interrelated, high risk, severe	professionally qualified and/or specialist professional

Fig. 2.1 Levels of assessment (Practitioners' Guide, p 42, DoH/SSI 1991).

This is a nightmare to interpret, since judgement has to be made early in the process. The pressure on parents is therefore to emphasise the initial difficulty, in order to obtain assessment by better-qualified staff and so secure the best possible response (Middleton 1997a). Assessment systems are not always so prescribed in children's services, but the practice of allocating a worker according to the initially-perceived level of complexity is widespread.

Since social workers understand that parents might play the system, they learn to allow for this, and thus increase the problem. Parents seeking to demonstrate the difficulties they face can either show the depth of their own stress by smoking, crying or shouting, or they can let the child's behaviour speak for itself. A child who is well behaved when the social worker visits may not be congratulated, but may hear his mother saying 'he's not normally like this'. An adult may understand the pressures to 'perform' as a rationing system demands, and choose whether or not to play along. It is less easy to explain to a child who is usually rewarded for being good.

This sets the child apart from other children, and her parents apart from other parents. It is a pernicious process in which it is difficult to intervene, since it is underpinned both by attitudes that devalue disabled children and by a cultural emphasis on self-reliance. Meeting the narrow eligibility criteria which will secure help means placing oneself outside of the self-help society, and into a dependent, resource-draining subgroup. Unlike the elderly, or those disabled in adulthood, there is no compensation factor in terms of having paid taxes, raised a family or served in wartime. In the UK these distinctions between 'deserving' and 'undeserving' are not made explicit, although I was struck on a visit to Israel by how much more open the authorities are in acknowledging the higher quality of service available to those citizens disabled in the defence of their country.

A disabled child is seen as non-contributing, not only in the present but also in the future. The pressure is therefore to invoke pity and hope for a sympathetic response. It is no coincidence that many of the services for disabled children are provided by charities.

The independent/statutory divide

The provision by specialist charities of services for children means that many children receive service, increasingly on a contractual basis from the statutory sector, on the basis of their diagnosis. Many charities are disability specific, such as the SCOPE schools for children with cerebral palsy or Lady Hoare social workers for those with arthritis. This is potentially very divisive and maintains a system whereby the child's medical condition is pre-eminent in determining health, educational and social needs. The segregation of services is reinforced by the impact of the internal market: the purchaser/provider split. Children who have complex or unusual needs are managed in specialist teams or contracted out of local authorities altogether. This might quite reasonably apply on an individual basis to children who are disruptive or display challenging behaviour, where both the voluntary and the private sector are used as a resource; it becomes less reasonable as a policy when applied on a *collective* basis to whole groups of children, such as those defined as 'disabled', whatever their individual circumstances might be. In some areas local authority social services contract out services for all 'disabled' children to Barnado's. I have argued elsewhere that the benefits of the undoubtedly high quality services offered in the independent sector have to be weighed against the disadvantages of stigma, patchiness and lack of accountability (Middleton, 1999).

Barnes argues that in British society seeking help from charities carries considerable stigma. 'In addition . . . eligibility has to be proven, provision is not a foregone conclusion and getting it usually takes time' (Barnes, 1994, p 59). This problem of stigma is not solved by shifting the terminology: changing from 'charity' to 'voluntary' to 'independent' to 'non-government organisation' or 'not for profit' is insufficient since it is associated with deep seated attitudes.

My local radio station bombarded its listeners for many weeks with an appeal for an individual disabled child, presumably with her parents' consent, and without apparent regard for what such publicity would mean for her self image. Whatever changes may be taking place in thinking at national and international level, this kind of activity is still widespread and many people fail to see anything wrong with it. Securing public donations means presenting an image of the recipients which encourages the donor to part with money; this image may not necessarily be compatible with accuracy, innovation in service or with the dignity of its subjects.

'Rights not charity' is widely promoted by the disability movement as an underlying value. If it is to become a direction for change, this has to involve not only the rejection by disabled people of their status as recipients, but also a rejection by donors of charity as the means of 'supporting' disabled children and their families through separate organisations. This involves a corresponding acceptance that disabled children have a right to their place in the queue for healthcare, to their seat in the classroom and to protection from abusers. It entails non-disabled people giving time and making room for disabled people alongside them in hospitals, surgeries, schools, play-groups, police stations and the law courts. It means major charities refocusing their power and influence to work towards the inclusion of disabled children in mainstream society, and eventually, of course, to their own redundancy in their present form.

The Spastics Society, now SCOPE, is a major provider of specialist education and social services for children and adults with cerebral palsy. The Spastics Society recognised its need to change to be more inclusive of its own service users by introducing the concept of individual membership in 1997. This was both to render itself more relevant to disabled people and also to loosen the connections with its extensive, parent-run local group network. The latter had come to be regarded as the reason for its lack of attraction to young people with cerebral palsy. Introducing the membership scheme owed a great deal to pressure from the disability rights movement for large charities to become organisations *of* rather than *for* disabled people.

It had already changed its name to SCOPE to symbolise its change of direction and its intention of breathing new life into the organisation. The hope of disability rights activists must be that the influence of more disabled members will be to emphasise collective campaigning and advocacy and reduce the emphasise on individual pathology. This means a change from the culture of the collection box towards the active involvement of disabled people in their own futures. This is a tall order, and only time will tell whether an old charity is a viable vehicle for such a movement. Time will also be the judge of whether an organisation accountable to individual adult members will prove any more effective in working in the interests of disabled children than one run by groups of parents.

An organisation run for and by disabled people, who are interested in promoting the rights of disabled people as equal citizens, is not compatible with the provision of segregated education and social services. This must mean that in the long term SCOPE faces a more radical choice about what sort of organisation it is.

Segregated services grow because of the absence of appropriate assistance in the mainstream. This should not excuse us from seeking the reasons for that absence, since it is probably because of an unwillingness to provide for certain groups. The history of services for people with AIDS is a more recent example of a service which developed separately because the main service users belonged to a stigmatised group (Miller & Murphy, 1998). Specialist facilities such as the Ankali project in Sydney, the Gay Men's Health Centre in New York and the Terence Higgins Trust in the UK grew up because the services in the mainstream health and welfare were inadequate and prejudiced against gay men. The results were good medical care and support, but at the expense of creating a veil of secrecy and mystique around the whole area of AIDS and HIV. As is the case with work with disabled children, sooner or later, someone will point out that those who have provided the specialist services have been keeping their expertise to themselves, and segregating people from normal health and welfare provision.

SCOPE and other charities therefore face a difficult choice, not least because there is often no current high quality alternative to the kind of education or social service which they and similar organisations provide. It would, of course, be far easier to argue for the ending of segregated services if they were of inherently poorer quality than those in the mainstream, but that is manifestly not the case. Nor is the statutory sector showing any desire to integrate. Indeed the statutory sector is actively supporting segregation by funding special schools and making contractual arrangements with the independent sector to undertake welfare services for particular client groups. Were major service providers in the independent sector to transmogrify into campaigning membership organisations overnight, it would leave another major gap in the welfare net. Nonetheless, the major specialist charities need to decide clearly what business they are in, and ask if providing service on the basis of physical or intellectual characteristics is compatible with a vision of an equal society.

This section is not an argument to abolish a mixed welfare system: not only would this be hopelessly impractical, but it would also deny the role which a vibrant independent sector can play in recognising and filling gaps in welfare and developing innovative services. The relationship between statutory and voluntary is not clear cut. In reality, most voluntary organisations receive funding both from the state and from public donations, a picture increasingly complicated by lottery funding. Statutory funding increasingly comes with service level agreements which to all intents and purposes can render a voluntary organisation part of the statutory system. On the other hand, many statutory services rely on appeals to provide what might be considered essential pieces of equipment, services or even staffing. Fund-raising for scanners, mini buses, school books, outings, holiday play-schemes and MacMillan nurses are all common.

I do not intend to try to disentangle these threads here. The overriding concern for disabled children is not who provides any particular welfare or educational service, but the basis on which children are assigned to different service providers. Mixed educational provision would not be a problem, as long as children were assigned to schools on the basis of educational and social need, rather than on the basis of an unrelated physical difference. Although they are often confused, this is quite a different matter from recognising that some children have specific learning difficulties, such as autism, which need to be addressed. Put simply, there is no justification for teaching maths to a child who cannot walk in a different school from one who can.

Using the same inclusive value base, there is no reason why an organisation could not raise money, say, to put on a children's pantomime, as long as they do so for all children. Taking this argument to its logical conclusion would mean not supporting the existence of charities which provide 'treats' exclusively for disabled children. This seems a small price to pay for inclusion. Addressing these issues involves more than tinkering with the benefits system: it entails a review of how we think, and what we mean by such terms as 'citizen'. This is considered in the last chapter.

SECTION II: Explanations for the exclusion of disabled children

The first section of this chapter has provided illustrative evidence of disadvantaging systems within health, education and social services. These are not areas divorced from the rest of life, and it would have been possible to present similar evidence from other spheres of life such as leisure or play. Rather than produce more evidence for disabling systems, securing improvement means moving on, first to seek explanations and then to suggest ways to effect change.

How far are oppressive structures – such as those described above – deeply rooted in history, and how far are they deliberately planned, created and consciously held in place? If the former is the case, and oppression is no more than unchallenged tradition or habit, then untangling the threads to explain where we are and how we arrived here would seem a logical precursor to an appeal for fair play.

If on the other hand, 'special need' is a conscious and deliberate means of promoting the wellbeing of the non-disabled majority, it has to be expected that simply appealing to a sense of fair play will never change things. Put simply, the dominant, non-disabled group may prefer things to remain as they are. Vested interests may develop on both sides of service provision, resulting in collusion between providers of specialist services and their opposite numbers in the mainstream.

If we are to understand why the oppressive system endures, it is not enough to understand the disadvantages endured by disabled children and adults (Oliver, 1990; Hirst & Baldwin, 1994; Barnes, 1994). These are well documented, as are narrative accounts of how they experience oppression (Morris, 1991, 1996b; Keith, 1994; Middleton, 1997b). There has to be more attention to the analysis and development of theoretical knowledge relating to children. In seeking explanations, therefore, connections have to be made between literature on children (which largely ignores disability issues) and literature on disability rights (which, with the exception of education, has largely focused on adults). There is still little to guide the enquiry into the complex interconnections between adult disability and disabled children.

We also need to appreciate the perceived advantages for the non-disabled in maintaining a two tier system, to challenge these beliefs and to offer other ways of organising services which are mutually beneficial. The majority stakeholders will not let go of what they believe works for them unless the alternative appears to be better.

One place to start this complicated analysis of why discrimination persists is to review the function of the welfare state and look at whose interests it serves. The evidence is that the British people support the idea of the welfare state. However, the enthusiasm for free and universal education, health and welfare operates within a society which has been bombarded with an ideology of self-interest for the last twenty years, ensuring continuing tensions between those who see themselves paying and those who consume. Yet self-interest and sound welfare systems are not incompatible. Good welfare services do not only benefit people directly; but their existence prevents economic and social upheaval by keeping a lid on distress. By and large society fails to invest adequately in the futures of disabled children. Since this makes poor economic sense, it seems obvious that their exclusion is not on economic grounds.

The Government's Social Exclusion Unit is not focusing on disabled children. Looking at the priorities the Government does set, and what it means by social exclusion, might provide an explanation for their omission. The Unit argues that exclusion arises from a combination of problems and cites unemployment, poor skills, low incomes, poor housing, high crime environments, bad health and family breakdown (Cabinet Office, 1997). All of these things adversely affect disabled people, as well as contributing to disablement, but the connection is not made either for disabled adults or children. The Government is focusing on those three areas where the target populations are more likely to engage in crime and drug abuse, and so contribute to community breakdown: 'truancy, street living and the worst estates'. This is not to imply that disabled children and adults cannot be delinquent, but to suggest that the usual perception of them as not being anti-social is one reason why they are so easy to ignore.

The survival of the fittest

The aim of health, education and welfare in this country has been, and still remains, to normalise disabled children as the route to inclusion in society rather than working to widen the boundaries of what is construed as acceptable and normal. This is a difficult issue, since most people would agree that it is better if a child is born with a minimum of impairments. However, this understanding has led to the exclusion of girls and boys who are not perfect, as well as to eugenic abortion. This means defining some children as 'disabled', often from a very early age. Children identify with different reference groups at different times but do not readily attribute disability labels to themselves (Allen, 1996). 'Disabled' is an administrative and social category which means that all children have to be one thing or another, either 'disabled' or not, rather than fitting somewhere into a continuum of ability. Such externally-driven pressures to define identity do not so much serve the individuals concerned as allow the rest of society to label its non-conformists.

Many disabled children will share with young gays and children in trans-racial foster placements the experience of having parents who are *not like them*, which can result in misunderstandings, feelings of failure and shame. Pressures to conform can take a higher priority than learning the coping strategies which they need to counter prejudice. Some never learn to cope and the resultant human misery is evidenced by both self-abuse and suicide.

This does not explain why societies cannot simply include all children in the first place. In the absence of a reasonable intellectual argument for exclusion, finding an explanation for its continuance may mean exploring more basic drives.

Is it possible that disabled girls and boys are excluded because they challenge deeper instincts which shape our relationships with each other and underpin the essentially hierarchical structures of society?

Survival of the species depends on the fittest individuals mating with each other and raising their young to the point of independence. Males have to be strong enough to fight off rivals, to hunt and provide for the dependent wife and child. Women have to attract and keep a man, at least as long as the children are dependent. Sex, parenthood, warfare (and its substitute, sport) are basic drives underpinning societal values of strength and beauty. Our language is peppered with sporting metaphors emphasising its essentially competitive nature.

We no longer live in the wild, compete with other animals or select our mates on the basis of their hunting skills. Yet the pursuit of beauty, strength and speed continues even though in many ways such attributes are redundant in relation to mankind's survival. Acknowledging that disabled people were equal would challenge these hierarchies based on physical characteristics.

Yet a deeply rooted belief that disabled people are worth less than non-disabled people may be a powerful motivator which underpins the way society operates. This is an unpalatable idea from which I suspect that most individuals would wish to distance themselves. Nonetheless, if such values do influence our thinking and behaviour, at both individual and societal levels, they are better openly discussed and understood.

The belief that some men are better than others is an ideology which has been used to justify massive racial and religious persecutions of different people. It provides reasons to persecute imperfect specimens *within* one's own tribe: millions of people, including those with disabilities, have suffered and died as a result. Fascist death camps represent the extreme manifestation of an attitude toward disabled people, but there are continuing echoes both in eugenics movements and in discussions about whether or not some lives are worth living (see Morris, 1991, Chapter 2, for a fuller account).

Less valued groups may be charged with undermining society or challenging 'family values'. Their exclusion is justified by the pro-mulgation of offensive myths which vilify and engender irrational hatreds. Most child murderers and molesters are heterosexual men, yet 'paedophiles' (meaning child abusers, not child lovers) and homo-sexuals have become very firmly linked in the popular imagination, just as black men have been stereotyped as sexually rapacious. It is argued that disabled people may have unprotected and irresponsible sex, produce a further generation of defective children, and so ultimately weaken the stock.

Tom Shakespeare quotes the following anecdote:

> 'there was these two people in the supermarket, and they were both wheelchair users, and they had a kiss, I don't know why they wanted to kiss in a supermarket, but they did, and somebody came up to them and said "Do you mind, its bad enough that there are two of you".'

(Shakespeare *et al.*, 1996, p 109)

During the writing of this book, it was suggested that this example was too extreme, and should be excluded in case it made the reader think of the inconvenience of wheelchairs blocking supermarket aisles rather than about eugenics. It may strike as perverse, but uncovering such thinking seemed to me a powerful reason to leave it in.

Compulsory sterilisation has been widely practised on the grounds that disabled people should not be allowed to have children. The opposite prejudice operates at the same time: disabled people are widely construed as asexual. Jazz, a disabled Jordanian woman quoted by Shakespeare (1996) claims that 'disability is a breed on its own, neither masculine or feminine' (p 60). They are stereotyped as of indeterminate gender and sexuality, not beautiful enough to attract a mate, strong enough to fight off the opposition nor interesting enough to their own sex to be gay. Nor are disabled men seen as presenting any sexual threat to women or children, an assumption which is both wrong and dangerous.

The 'defects' of homosexuals and disabled people allow both groups to be widely discriminated against as imperfect human beings. There are differences, one of which is that a visibly disabled child cannot so easily hide from a world which disapproves of him. Disabled girls and boys are more likely to be seen as weak or tragic than perverse or deviant. This construction leaves disabled children objectified as victims able to play little part in their own destiny. It has excused researchers and service providers alike from including them. Research concerning disability, perhaps following the availability of funding, is dominated by medically-driven studies where disabled children are not seen as useful informants. Priestley notes that the medical agenda has also unduly influenced much social research which has focused on particular disabling conditions and how to 'handle them':

> 'It has become common practice in social research with disabled children to pick your impairment first and ask questions later.'
>
> (Priestley, 1998a, p 209)

Sport is a highly prized activity, in which success is well rewarded and applauded. A high value is placed on physical perfection measured in terms of speed, strength, endurance, grace, style and the ability to fight. Disability represents the opposite. It is conceptualised as unhealthy. A child with an abnormality symbolises the failure of medical science. Disability is associated with poverty, poor health, inadequate education and imperfect science. Sports stars carry our dreams while disabled people carry our fears.

Disabled people are less likely to play the sort of games where touching the rest of the team or man-handling the opposition are expected. As such they are not conceptualised as serious participants in the most popular sports. Disabled competitors are bombarded with remarks about how brave or exceptional they are. While the Paralympics have gone a long way to help society recognise that having an impairment does not preclude competition at an international level, why are weight-lifters who cannot walk in a totally separate games from those who can?

There are many ways in which 'playing fields could be levelled' to allow disabled people better opportunities, in sport and in other arenas such as education and employment. It makes sense economically and socially to include as many people as possible in society, and yet we do not do so. Is it because of resistance to the idea that disabled people might win and disturb the 'natural' order of things? The evidence indicates that people are happy to let disabled people play sports and games, but only on their terms and only so long as they do not perform better than non-disabled competitors.

Casey Martin is described by the sporting press as a brilliant young golfer (*Guardian*, 4th February 1998). His disability means he needs to use a golf cart. The US PGA is adamant that no-one should be exempt from its rule that walking the usual five miles is an essential part of tournament golf and that allowing Martin to use a cart would give him an unfair advantage. The issue here is not about the essential fairness or otherwise of the competition, but the fear that a man with only one good leg might actually beat non-disabled golfers.

The 'order of things' may not be 'natural' but it is deeply entrenched in our social relationships. Sport is widely understood as ritualised warfare in which individuals, communities and nations establish pecking orders without resorting to actual bodily harm but we also engage in social rituals to establish and maintain dominance (Knipe & Maclay, 1973). Young boys determine who is boss by pushing and shoving but the group will be confused by a blind child. How manly will it seem for the top boy to push a blind child about? Should they simply exclude, or perhaps acquire 'helper' status by serving as a guide? Adults still resort to real fighting, but much hierarchical behaviour now depends on other cues. Dominant people sit in bigger chairs, are allowed to slap their subordinates patronisingly on the back, expect them to drop their gaze and get out of the way when they walk about. Men and women work out whose turn it is to speak, who is making the decisions and who is making the tea by a series of subtle gestures and social cues from which disabled people can easily be excluded since they involve physical indicators such as height, personal space or body language. A blind person will miss the eye contacts and cannot be intimidated with a firm look. A wheelchair user cannot so easily be slapped on the back. He is already sitting too low to confront, and he cannot be tripped up. A deaf person may translate the words but miss the message in the tone of voice.

All of these factors skew behaviours and signals which are otherwise socially understood. Disabled people present a threat to established patterns of interaction. Worse than that, they do so as imperfect beings.

High status individuals resent having to change their behaviour to accommodate and include those of lower rank.

Shakespeare and his colleagues argue that accommodating to other people's values compounds low self esteem and suggest that 'another approach would be to educate the non-disabled world about the oppression of disabled people rather than finding ways ... of making ourselves more acceptable' (Shakespeare *et al.*, 1996). But how realistic is it to expect disabled people to occupy the moral high ground? The chances are that disabled people as individuals are as intolerant, immoral, and imperfect as people in general. However a social *movement* can shift thinking and attitudes beyond individual shortcomings and toward collective ideals.

The question then becomes: What sort of campaign for inclusion would ultimately enhance the quality of disabled people's lives? How far do you exert pressure to join in society as it exists, as opposed to expecting society to make changes both to accommodate difference and to examine its values? Do you stop the games or change the rules?

In one respect the struggle for equality for disabled people is intertwined with the technological revolution, which can equalise people by removing physical, communication and even skill barriers between them. Disabled girls and boys too could be higher, faster, richer and better informed provided the rest of us are prepared to change the rules. It seems we are not.

Disabled people are not expected to go to war, even in separate units, and even though the high reliance on technology in modern warfare would make it possible. Much of warfare is posturing, and represents an individual, group or society demonstrating itself as stronger than another. If disabled people are not seen as whole men, they are less likely to be expected to participate in such rituals. Becoming disabled threatens not simply physical wellbeing, but an individual's identity as a man (or woman).

The prejudice about 'manhood' can extend to becoming a father of a disabled child. As a social worker with the Spastics Society in the 1980s I worked with a number of army families where men serving overseas had been sent back to Britain with their families after fathering a child with cerebral palsy. This not only jeopardised military career prospects by limiting opportunity for the man in question, but lowered his status in the eyes of other soldiers. In what is a very macho culture, fathering a disabled child can reflect adversely on the manliness of the father.

Technological revolutions which diminish the value of physical strength have not eradicated the value placed on it by men seeking to dominate others. Brute force still intimidates many women and children in the home, and in residential establishments. Some children copy and perpetuate such behaviour in streets and school playgrounds. Violence may be condemned as immoral and illegal but it receives implicit approval since it matches what is rewarded, applauded and admired in men's behaviour elsewhere; in their struggle for equality and for inclusion, disabled people pose a threat to long established sets of values.

While there have been undeniable advances in thinking, too many men and women still subscribe to the illogical view that men's greater physical strength makes them *better* than women and gives them the right to make most of the decisions. The dominance of male decision-makers is still the pattern in most large organisations, and in the government. In the same way too many disabled and non-disabled people retain a view not only that being able-bodied is better, but that able-bodied people are better equipped to manage, give advice or make decisions by virtue of the absence of impairment. A simple example is the 'Does he take sugar?' syndrome, where non-disabled carers are expected to answer on behalf of disabled people.

If disabled children are considered as inferiors, they can be more readily pitied, patronised, bullied, abused or excluded rather than educated and treated as equals, sexually or socially.

Morris's explanation (Morris, 1991) for the exclusion of disabled people is fear and denial of *'frailty, vulnerability, morbidity and arbitrariness of human experience'*. She argues that the general culture is the poorer for ignoring their experience. We isolate those who are disabled, old or ill because they are not like us, but remind us of what we might become. This argument may help to explain why the price of acceptance for excluded groups is usually for them to become more like the majority rather than for the majority to take steps to widen the boundaries of inclusion. Conductive education was founded on the premise that children should be able to walk before they could attend school. Enormous emphasis is placed on deaf children to learn to speak, an expectation which is not balanced by that of encouraging hearing children to sign. Sticks and wheelchairs as aids to mobility carry a stigma not shared by ski-poles or bicycles.

Fear of difference has been advanced as an explanation for many prejudices, and words such as homophobia and xenophobia are used to describe such fears. More recently, Islamophobia has been documented and described, although fear of Muslims is nothing new. The authors of the Runnymede Report describe Islamophobia in terms of four overlapping aspects: *exclusion*, from government, employment and responsibility; *discrimination*, as in health and education; *prejudice* in the media and in everyday conversation; and *violence*, ranging from verbal abuse to physical assault (Runnymede Trust, 1997, p 11).

What is striking about this model is how easily it translates to the oppression of other groups, such as women, homosexuals or disabled people. But what is also striking is how inadequate 'fear' is as an explanation. If 'phobia' were an explanation, then educating people about difference – whether in terms of race, culture, lifestyles or physical appearances – would be sufficient to end oppression. This is clearly not the case.

People, organisations, and races do not disadvantage others simply out of fear and ignorance, but are positively motivated to discriminate because it is thought to be advantageous. Deaf people have long sought recognition as an oppressed linguistic minority which could cease if future generations learned their language. All hearing school children *could* learn sign language, as was suggested earlier and may even find it fun. This would not only enhance their own abilities to communicate with deaf children and adults, but also with other hearing people in noisy environments, across distances and across international boundaries. On the face of it there is nothing to lose. Sign language is rarely taught not because it is ineffective but because it is associated with a devalued group. It may be more than that because communication gives people power. Teaching all children to sign would give them a power beyond that of most adults. The levels of discomfort engendered in the adult population by whole generations of children communicating in a different language would be enormous, mirroring perhaps some of the discomfort currently being experienced by computer illiterate adults whose children surf the Internet. Teaching sign language to young children would threaten the power basis of the dominant adult, hearing majority. Nor, unlike selling computers and software, would there be any obvious profits to be made.

The essential reasonableness of the explanations for discrimination which are based on fear, ignorance and stigma disregard the unreasonableness of much of human adult behaviour. Worse still, it is an unreasonableness which is encouraged by the current mores of self reliance and individual rights. Our societal expectation is that we should compete, which means getting on *at the expense of others*. This means creating and maintaining hierarchical structures based on power and on status. In this respect the playground bully is merely rehearsing for adult life, whether at work or in the home.

Conclusion

Disadvantage is not created solely by impairment but by the way society reacts to it. The processes which create special needs frequently have to be undone later in life by processes such as normalisation, rehabilitation, access education or assertiveness training. In the meantime, non-disabled adults are undergoing 'disability awareness training'. A disabled child has the same needs as any other, although they may have to be met in different ways. Despite this obvious fact, we have created an elaborate system of segregated education and welfare which means that a child with an impairment is more likely to experience discrimination than to enjoy equality.

Such exclusion is justified in many people's minds by a view that disabled children are non-contributing and do not merit the same equality of treatment nor investment in their education since they will not grow up to take responsibilities as citizens. This can be a self-fulfilling prophecy: a disabling childhood would place children at a disadvantage in the employment market even if the market itself were fair. Furthermore making human, or even animal, rights conditional on taking responsibility denies the duty of care in a civilised society to protect vulnerable individuals and groups from aggression, abuse and injustice.

The dominant majority continues to resist change, not simply because of ignorance or fear of difference, but because people who enjoy exercising power over others do not surrender it lightly. This applies at any level in the hierarchy. On an individual level, it is more often those who have low status in their organisations who belittle and bully disabled children. Unfortunately these are often people in positions of trust, who have direct access to children and can exercise power over them: bus drivers, porters, care staff, classroom assistants, and nurses for example.

Improving the wellbeing of disabled children therefore involves changes at all levels, from societal attitudes to the training of key individuals.

Chapter 3

Conceptual Frameworks

In trying to understand the processes involved in change, I have found each of the following conceptual frameworks helpful and offer them not as blueprints, since each is flawed in its way, but as an aid to thought.

Improving the situation for disabled children involves changes throughout health, education and welfare systems. Micro and macro systems interact with each other. Whilst making changes at a personal level will not *in itself* produce change in an organisation, the converse is equally true. Organisational change will not work effectively unless personal behaviours change as well, whether the change is voluntarily or otherwise. The complications of personal and organisational interactions across and within organisations need more than one conceptual framework within which to analyse change. The next two chapters make use of three such frameworks. The 'SEAwall' conceptualises difficulties in terms of barriers. The steps of the NVQ Model illustrate the different levels at which change must occur, while the Jigsaw emphasises the interdependence of pieces of the picture.

The SEAwall

In discussing organisational difficulties faced by disabled people, John Swain and his colleagues conceptualise a barrier which they graphically describe as a SEAwall of institutional discrimination (Figure 3.1) where Structural, Environmental and Attitudinal bricks are cemented together by ideologies of 'normality' and 'independence' (Swain *et al.*, 1998).

This is an extremely useful way of conceptualising the discriminatory barriers faced by disabled people. As a model for change the SEAwall is limited in being two dimensional and undynamic, suggesting that any progress is dependent on the whole wall being dismantled at some point in time. It leads to a revolutionary model for change which can devalue the contribution of smaller, or pre-figuring, changes and as such can seem an overwhelming challenge. As a model it is probably of more use to service users than professionals, disabled or not, since it implies challenging a system from outside rather than whittling away from

	Cemented by ideologies of normality and independence →		
Attitudinal	Cognitive prejudice: assumptions about the (in)abilities, emotional responses, needs of disabled people	Emotional prejudice: fear	Behavioural prejudice: individual practice and praxis	
Environmental	Disablist language	Institutional policies, organisation, rules and regulations	Professional practices: assessment, care management	Inaccessible physical environments
Structural	Hierarchical power relations and structures: disempowerment of disabled people	The denial of human, social and welfare rights	Structural inequalities: poverty	

Fig. 3.1 The SEAwall of institutional discrimination (from Swain *et al.*, 1998, p.6.)

within. It will certainly appeal more to those who envisage challenging oppression as a fight rather than an incremental process of persuasion.

The NVQ model

Those who favour a persuasive model, and put their faith in education and reason as a route to change, may prefer the image of a series of steps based on the competency model of National Vocational Qualifications, where earlier skills and knowledge are built up into a bigger picture.

Level 7 Societal change
Level 6 Political change
Level 5 Organisational change
Level 4 Professional change
Level 3 Personal change
Level 2 Not making things worse
Level 1: Awareness

(Middleton 1997b)

This emphasises the essential underpinning of attitudes and illustrates the various levels at which change has to be effected. It carries the disadvantage of assuming that, like real steps, these levels must be climbed in sequence rather than faced simultaneously like the SEAwall. There is some truth in that assumption as an individual journey, but it is less helpful when addressing oppression as a collective problem. It can lead to a rational model of evolutionary and logical change which denies the often bloody and disorderly reality of the change process. A belief that attitudes must be changed before changes in procedures, management or rules can be implemented is a trap which can effectively prevent any progress. Many organisational efforts at change have not got past 'awareness raising'.

Disabled people may not be prepared to wait for their rights until everyone else is convinced of the justice of the case. In contrast to the SEAwall it is a model which may be of more relevance to professionals, both disabled and non-disabled, than to service users since it implies an internal change process and is based on a willingness to learn.

The 3-D jigsaw

A jigsaw is a picture which is composed of many pieces, of different sizes and shapes. Some are more important than others. Some may be missing, or in someone else's hands. Adding another piece can change the way the whole thing looks. An ordinary jigsaw is too flat as a concept, but a three dimensional one better illustrates the complexity of the puzzle, since it is never possible to see it all at once.

The reader should imagine themselves moving around a huge sculpture of multi-coloured interlocking shapes. Like any sculpture, much is in the eye of the beholder and it looks different depending on the perspective from which it is viewed. Unlike the sculptures we are used to, however, this one is both dynamic and eternally incomplete. Any of the interlocking shapes can be taken out at any time and their colour or pattern changed. In such a sculpture, changing one piece not only alters that section of the picture, but influences the way in which we see the whole. Things might not fit so well as before and have to be altered in their turn. While it is tempting to pull it all apart and start again from scratch, there is also the fear that this will make things worse.

The main pieces of the puzzle are the politics and contextual environment of health and welfare services, the service users, families, friends, organisational culture and practices, 'special needs' in welfare and education, personal attitudes, relationships and professional practice.

It is only possible to describe the pieces of this puzzle one at a time. Yet change in one dimension will usually only work or last if something or other elsewhere in the system also changes. This does not deny the value of individual contributions nor the worth of small steps (indeed, both are essential) but it recognises their interdependence with other factors.

The next two chapters provide some suggestions for professional and organisational changes. Many of the changes do not apply solely to services for disabled children, but relate to sound service provision. I have chosen to focus much illustrative material on single sectors, since a 'Cook's tour' around health, welfare and education in each of these next two chapters could easily become repetitive, as well as too thin to be helpful.

Chapter 4

The Professional and Personal Challenge

'Despite imperatives to integrate services it is hard to rid ourselves of the belief that disabled children need something different or special. Whether we are disabled or not we have all grown up being fed that belief. If we are not disabled we have been fed the belief that we are better; that we can help by popping money into tins; that disabled children are not like us. If we are disabled we have been fed the belief that we are a disappointment, at best, or a burden, or that it would be better if we were more normal.'

(Contributor to Suffolk Social Services seminar to service providers, Bury St Edmunds, 13th November 1996)

Introduction

The first part of this book discussed the situation in which disabled children grow up, and illustrated it from the perspective of a group of disabled young people. It has presented three main arguments.

(1) The current welfare system in the UK is both fragmented and discriminatory. It creates disadvantage for children who are physically different, and it does so by conceptualising them as having 'special needs'. Disabled children are excluded because the boundaries of 'normality' are drawn too narrowly.

(2) The exclusion of disabled children is defended on the grounds that their inclusion would disadvantage the majority of non-disabled children. The ethos of self help and independence has permeated society, and finds a ready enough echo in the disability movement, yet as long as it is believed that one section's future may only be secured by sacrificing another group, the survival of the fittest will not be left to chance. The right of disabled children to equality of opportunity, access to welfare and healthcare services is sacrificed in order that the majority of non-disabled children are not held back, kept waiting or drained of resources.

(3) Countering the above argument by rational debate will be insufficient to achieve social justice, since maintaining the inequality of disabled children enables many non-disabled people to exercise

their power and feel better about themselves. The issue is therefore emotional as much as it is intellectual.

The aims of change are therefore:

(1) To create an inclusive welfare system which ends the discriminatory concept of 'special need'. This means directing education to achieve learning, and health and welfare services to deal with real medical or social problems rather than making assumptions about need based on physical characteristics. It might prove a useful exercise for organisations to try rewriting their information materials without recourse to the word 'special'.

(2) To counter the argument that inclusion will harm the non-disabled majority and work toward equalising opportunity.

(3) To address the psychological issues which support an oppressive hierarchical structure. This involves attitudes towards children, disability and disabled children.

(4) To counter social exclusion by extending the boundaries of health, social and educational systems so that they include all groups of children within mainstream provision.

It follows from these aims that simply presenting isolated examples of 'good practice' is insufficient since the changes require a fundamental review of the welfare system. In order to achieve this, organisations will have to reappraise their own services in the light of legislative demand, current value systems, sound childcare principles, and the views of disabled children as far as they are known. These are ambitious goals.

Dismantling oppression is not simply an organisational challenge. More fundamentally it is a professional and personal one. So before we can even begin to deal with changing organisations, it is essential that each individual in a position to influence change addresses their own values and attitudes about the place of disabled children in society.

Attitudes and values

Addressing attitudes and values is not a once-and-for-all event, but a continual process of appraisal, with an awareness that there are others travelling the road sometimes behind and sometimes ahead of us, and moving at different speeds. It entails having an understanding of what oppression is, what structural unfairness feels like and what it does to people. It helps to have a vision of what might constitute a less oppressive society, so that some mechanisms can be devised for moving forward. In the case of disabled children this means ending fear of disability and moving toward a society enriched by diversity. This is more complicated than valuing different race, gender or sexuality because disabled children have an impairment which, without any discrimination from society, may cause inconvenience, pain, discomfort, tiredness, sickness, ill health or premature death. Most reasonable people would prefer that children were not impaired. This makes discrimination against disabled children and adults essentially different from discrimination against those groups which are different but unimpaired. It means valuing the child while accepting not only the impairment is permanent but that it is a part of them.

This is not to suggest that these lines are simple. The case has been argued that other groups are imperfect and they are discriminated against as a result. Women have been conceptualised as incomplete men; weaker, emotional and less intelligent. Similarly children are sometimes seen as incomplete adults. Black people have been seen as inferior to white people, and homosexuality has been widely thought of as a sickness. On the other hand, many people who are unimpaired, for example some short people, count themselves as 'disabled' because of the way society reacts to their difference.

When asked what they would change if they had a magic wand, some of the disabled students did not choose to change themselves physically. Only one expressed this in terms of fear of being able to see; the others were content with themselves as they were. This is difficult for most non-disabled people to accept, but it has to underpin thinking if any meaningful alliance between disabled and non-disabled is to work.

Wanting to change might reflect discrimination and a recognition that some groups seem to have a better time. Girls may want to be boys because boys have more fun; gay teenagers want to be straight because they want to fit in. Black children may want to be white because white children get on better with the teacher; children want to be grown ups because grown ups get to stay up later, and so on. If children feel all right about themselves, they will not want to change. Being non-disabled would mean being a different person. Disabled people who declare that they would not wish to change are making a powerful political statement that disabled people are as good as anyone else.

Many adults with impairments would not choose to alter their bodies even if it were possible. This can extend to parenthood and wishes for children. Lyn Barnes, a social worker with deaf people, posed the following question to me:

> 'If genetic engineering could screen out hearing children, would deaf parents be allowed to select to have deaf children only? How do you feel about that?'

> (personal communication)

Working with disabled children means accepting all the difficulties and personal dilemmas that arise for the children, their parents, siblings and for the professionals who work with them. It is an emotionally charged world in which there will always be someone with strong opinions who believes that others have less right than they have to their views, feelings, or involvement. The child can be the least powerful of all. Professional detachment can get a little difficult: where disabled children are concerned, professional skills, personal relationships and an understanding of ways to counter discrimination are part of the picture. It is unlikely that professional workers will travel far along the road unless they first take the time to acknowledge and understand their own feelings.

> 'Canadian farmer Robert Latimer was convicted of second degree murder for killing his 12 year old daughter to spare her the pain of her "worsening cerebral palsy", and sentenced to two years imprisonment less one day. It was described as a mercy killing, and the usual mandatory life sentence for murder was set aside by the judge as being "cruel".
>
> The decision was condemned by disability rights groups as supporting the "Barnyard ethics" of killing the weak.'

> (*Guardian*, 2nd December 1997)

Attitudes are important not only because they underpin and shape an individual's behaviour, but also because they are picked up by others. Non-disabled pupils easily pick up a teacher's attitude toward a disabled pupil (DoE, 1989). It is also worth reminding ourselves that because most professionals are non-disabled there remains a shortage of positive role models in all professional groups.

Professionals attempting to change themselves or others may first need to recognise that, having been educated in a disablist society, they may have developed disablist attitudes. This applies whether or not they themselves have a disability. One of the effects of oppression is that negative attitudes can be internalised by members of minority groups. Professionals may value disabled children less than those who are not disabled, regard them as objects of pity, or fail to notice their uniqueness. Disabled children are often viewed through the lens of their disabling condition and assumptions made about them on the basis of their physical characteristics. Realisation that they hold unhelpful attitudes can be a painful journey for those who consider themselves caring, tolerant and in favour of a society based on principles of equality or social justice. This can engender guilt, which some disability activists might encourage, but such a response is not conducive to constructive change. It is more helpful to develop an understanding of the mechanisms through which we learn disablist attitudes and the means by which they are reinforced. In this way we can acknowledge, resist and revise them.

Awareness trainers use checklists of statements designed to highlight attitudes which may be unrecognised, seem unimportant or even be subconscious. Running through these kind of statements can help identify difficult or ambivalent feelings which are better discussed in the open than left negatively to affect behaviour and thoughts.

Working with disabled children

In discussing cultural factors in child protection, Channer and Parton refer to 'reconstructed racism' which can lead to failure to act (Channer & Parton, 1990, p 112). Workers faced with a black child can behave differently and inappropriately if they get too caught up by the fear of offending cultural norms and in doing so deskill themselves and endanger the child. Arguably, middle class social workers may miss neglect or abuse within working class families if they condone poor childcare on the grounds that standards are different, or out of sympathy for the plight of parents. This is quite different from understanding and trying to help families cope within situations of poverty or poor housing. It is not an easy balance to maintain. (See Stevenson, 1998, for a discussion of these difficulties.)

There are similar dynamics of professional inaction where disabled children are concerned. Sympathy for parents does not obviate the duty to protect the child. A great deal of unhelpful mystique has developed around working with disabled children, across education, social services and healthcare. This is fed both by disability 'experts' who wish to preserve their professional turf, and by those other workers who are content not to extend their remit to cover disabled children. Disabled children are disadvantaged by the maintenance of this exclusive system. Parents and grandparents can catch the same fear, and feel deskilled when the child is diagnosed as having some sort of disability.

Garnett (1996) describes how

> 'the world of special and remedial education created its own professional mystique and this encouraged teachers in the mainstream to consider themselves unqualified and unskilled to deal with such children.'
>
> (p 118)

Barnes (1994) argues that many teaching courses offered to those wishing to extend their remit to work with disabled children tend to

> 'adhere to the traditional individualistic medical model of disability, and hence are unlikely to change the prejudices and perceptions of those who attend them.'
>
> (p 60)

Stakes and Hornby (1997) conclude that despite improvements in both the status of the special education specialist and extra resources for training,

> 'many teachers continue to feel a lack of confidence in working with pupils with "special educational needs", a term used to distinguish and divide children into two distinct groups.'
>
> (p 130)

A more helpful model would be one of a continuum of learning needs into which all children slotted.

This enduring mystique continues to provide the teaching profession and local authorities with a ready and plausible excuse for not including children who are difficult to teach. The NUT, which supports the requirements of the 1976 Education Act and the principles of the Warnock Report (DES 1978) both of which 'encourage' integration, has rightly and consistently called for more resources in terms of professional development to implement such integration (Stakes & Hornby, 1997). However any such extra investment will only help if it starts from the basic premise that sound educational principles apply to all children.

Similar mystiques have arisen with childcare workers who often deal only with non-disabled children. The problem is exacerbated by a corresponding fear of child protection on the part of many disability workers (Middleton, 1996). This fear is too often fed by workers in both fields seeking to preserve their own status as experts. This has led in some areas to a mutual stand off, which is illustrated in Fig. 4.1.

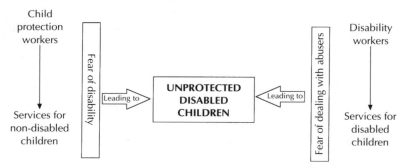

Fig. 4.1   Disabled children: excluded citizens? (Middleton, 1998a)

The integrative intent of the Children Act 1989 meant many social workers from disability backgrounds came to child protection work for the first time. Conversely, child protection workers were asked to investigate and take responsibility for disabled children. Many found difficulty in extending their respective remits. Social workers in general want to help, to be needed, to fix things and to be effective, but they differ in what they mean by these things.

Research with workers from both protection and disability fields indicated each have their own mystiques and cultures (Middleton, 1996). Disability specialists believe that they are more flexible than child protection workers: friendly, supportive, and less hemmed in by controlling managers. They stereotype the child protection workers as hidebound by procedure and less people-skilled. The disability worker sees child protection as essentially risky, and requiring a macho approach by someone who enjoys the rush of adrenaline which dealing with crisis can bring. Child protection is about having to 'get it right'. Disability workers believe they are less likely to get the necessary training or practice, in terms of numbers of cases, and will lack both peer group support and management back up. This results in a lack of confidence in tackling child protection.

Disability-focused organisations, and even many childcare organisations outside the statutory sector, also lack confidence in managing child abuse for many of the same reasons. In addition they find it hard to believe that carers for disabled children could actually perpetrate abuse. Disability workers do not come across the same extent of abuse as child protection workers, and may find it hard to accept that most abusers do not have horns and tails, but are ordinary people just like them. There is a mental hurdle to overcome in accepting the possibility that foster carers, hospital porters, taxi drivers, childcare workers, nurses, volunteer helpers as well as parents themselves commit abuse. It is an even bigger mental hurdle to believe that a highly dangerous minority of people actually seek that kind of work so that they can abuse, and that they may well be cunning, use different names, and work with one another. Nor will most have criminal records or be on paedophile registers. Professionals in the caring business cannot afford complacency.

Rightly, disability workers value relationships, but in some cases the relationship can become an end in itself. In an adult world it can easily focus on a dialogue with parents, rather than children, and worse still, on the worker's own need to be needed. The focus on parents means the child can easily become cast as the problem.

Yet child protection workers can feel helpless when faced with a disabled child. Like teachers and general practitioners who lack experience of disability, they experience a feeling of being de-skilled. They cannot communicate by their normal method. They do not understand the impairment, and may wrongly attribute behaviours which would otherwise alert them to the possibility of abuse. They may feel sympathetic toward the parents having to deal with a disabled child and therefore reluctant to entertain the idea they may abuse. Also, if 'rescue' becomes necessary, there is often nowhere obvious to take a disabled child for refuge. It is very easy to conclude that this is specialist work for which they have neither training nor resources.

Child protection workers may share the same disablist values which permeate society. Less value is placed on the child, and therefore less value is placed on their protection. Child protection workers may also get distracted by the fact that they cannot *cure* the disability, even though that is not being asked of them. In their case, making the situation better means doing something about the abuse.

Within the health service it is not uncommon for children with long term disabling conditions to be managed from acute hospital wards. While diagnosis and the prediction of disabling conditions has become much more sophisticated and accurate in the last 30 years or so, it still remains the case that much remains unknown in terms of prognosis and long term outcomes. The long term management of childhood disability needs to take account of the incremental nature of its revelation; the different developmental profiles of individual children; the influence of environment, the emotional and psychological effect of the family situation and the sheer unpredictability of childhood.

This all indicates that it is preferable to manage the situation for a disabled child on a long term basis within the family and community, rather than long distance from the acute paediatric ward. However there are similar issues about professional mystique: hospital-based professionals remain reluctant to 'let go', despite the fact that community-based professionals such as health visitors and community nurses have a far better chance of understanding and working with the family and community dynamics. The distinct skills needed to work within people's homes, as opposed to on wards, are now becoming more widely recognised. Within nursing training, for example, 'community pathways' are now offered as one year post diploma courses. This recognition of the value of a holistic approach could usefully be followed by an erosion of the current unhelpful divisions between 'sick' nurses and those for 'learning disability', as if the categories were mutually exclusive.

Despite the limitations of medical science to 'cure', doctors retain their credibility as experts often beyond the medical arena, and many do not hesitate to pass opinions about education. One student from Preston described how the doctor attending her special school suggested she would be better off at a residential school since it specialised in her particular condition: cerebral palsy.

> 'Mum would not have chosen for me to go to residential school. She found it incredibly difficult but she is also the type of person really who thinks the doctor knows best.'

In a satirical piece for the British Medical Journal, a paediatrician identifies two characteristics of his medical colleagues : an unfortunate combination of arrogance and ignorance.

> 'The segregation of Differents creates additional problems. Few people feel comfortable with them and few of my medical colleagues seem to know much about them ... some of my colleagues tend to look on my interest in this area in a rather patronising way.'

> (Graves, 1993)

Graves goes on to comment that many doctors tend to patronise disabled adults and children, do not treat them as equals, and rarely seek their opinion. This failure to involve children (or their parents) as equals in the management of their condition or situation is not confined to the medical profession. As described earlier, disabled children serve the interests of many individuals for whom having someone to pity, control or simply look down on serves a purpose. The growth of 'expertise' around disability is one aspect of this. It leads to staff who talk patronisingly about 'children like these', which is usually followed by something along the lines of: 'will always need ... something special'. Graves (1993) refers to such people as the Categoricans, a society which employs 'labellers' to seek out and separate those who are different. Students on placement can find themselves influenced by attitudes of permanent staff. Nursing training was described to me recently as learning by 'sitting next to Nelly'. This hit-and-miss system has now been replaced by more formal structures, but Nelly may still retain considerable influence as the custodian of 'how it's done here', which makes it essential to ensure that Nelly is an effective role model.

Professional unwillingness to listen supports, and is supported by, vested interests, which may seek to maintain existing systems, however much hard evidence points towards change. Jay writes of the 'incredible furore and attacks' which the 'simple and common-sense recommendations' of the Jay report created among health service employees despite the massive amount of evidence of abuse within the hospital system (Jay, 1996, p 44).

Despite these examples it is important not to overstate this situation. The welfare/healthcare relationship is a complex one, and in contrast to the examples given, many professionals are actively working toward partnership, engaging service users and resisting those changes arising from the ideology of the marketplace which they see as disadvantaging the more vulnerable in society. They represent workers who have not succumbed to the current pessimism within welfare, characterised by feelings of helplessness in the face of managerial control (Middleton, 1998c).

Searing (1998) writes of the changes she has noticed in 27 years work in childcare :

> 'In the 1970s I was working within a child care framework primarily concerned with supportive services to families and child placement. In the 1990s I have found myself working within a child protection system with many complex systems for controlling scarce resources, where traditional child care work seems to be downgraded.'

> (p 4)

Her attitude is not untypical of social workers who believe that the values of care management are undermining skills in working with children and families in a supportive fashion. There is a growing body of writing and research which would support a such a view (Parton, 1997; Gardner, 1998).

Changing professional behaviour

Having identified professionals as the key to making adequate provision for disabled children, ways need to be found to identify and enhance appropriate skills and helpful attitudes. There are two strands to this: first, for existing workers, and second, in training the next generation. This does not mean abandoning existing skills in nursing, teaching or child protection, but having confidence in them and extending them to cover all children. Asking some searching questions about their practice will identify what differences the presence of a disabled child makes, without losing the key knowledge and skills of their professional training. Thus teachers need to remain alive to sound principles about how children learn. Theories on this may change, but there is essentially little difference between how disabled children learn and how non-disabled children learn. Some take longer than others, and may need different methods of transmitting and recording information, but the essential lessons are the same. Children learn better if they are interested, discover things for themselves, see the relevance of what they are being taught, have lessons reinforced and so on. All children benefit from individual attention, and are motivated by the interest and encouragement of their teachers. Success breeds success, so it is important for teachers to reward rather than discourage by highlighting failure.

A medical practitioner needs to examine critically the reasoning that underlies any decision on the treatment of a disabled child, and to ask some key questions before choosing a course of action. 'Would I consider this intervention if the child were not disabled? Would I offer something else to an able-bodied child? Is the difference a medical one related to the disabling condition, or does it reflect prejudice about the rights of the child to particular treatment? Is this treatment cosmetic? If so, how much does it reflect the fears of the parents rather than the needs of the child? Is it painful? Will it improve the child's ability to do things he or she wants to do? Is this the best time for this treatment? Can it wait until the child is old enough to be consulted? Is it interfering with the child's education? Am I refusing treatment for this child for medical reasons? If not, what is my justification?'

Childcare workers need to value their childcare skills and apply them to their practice with disabled children. It is still too common for sound childcare to be over-ridden in the search for solutions for disabled children (Middleton, 1996). Signs and signals which would normally alert a worker to the possibility of abuse should be investigated in the usual way, rather than ignored as part of the disabling condition. This would, for example, mean requiring an explanation for bruising around the mouth, for explicit sexual behaviour inappropriate to a child's age, or sudden weight loss. Bruises on a child's leg are not 'caused' by callipers, but by roughness in the way they are put on.

'Challenging behaviour', which was once translated for me as 'eloquence', may be an attempt to communicate unhappiness. The usual safeguards in terms of information, review visits and inspection should apply to disabled children placed away from home (Morris, 1997; Utting, 1997).

Social workers who are already skilled in child protection work need to widen their expertise. They should be alert to the differences that the disability may be making, not simply to the child's development and behaviour, but to the relationships within the family. The quality of relationships within the family is more important than its structure. A crucial question to untangle may be how far, if at all, the presence of a disabled child is creating extra pressure, and how far the child is being scapegoated for pressures that might well exist anyway, such as problems at work, or financial hardship. The child may be in danger either way, but the solutions are not the same. Stresses in the home can arise from such matters as lack of sleep or fights about feeding. Externally, parents may report the wear and tear of dealing with hospitals and clinics. Much needless pressure can relate to poor or absent service provision, including education, where commonly parents have to 'fight' or beg for what should be standard services. In addition, stress can be created by ignorant neighbours or work colleagues. Within the family, reactions to the child and the disability need to be explored. Do they hate the disabling condition, or do they hate the child? Can they separate the two? Do they want the child dead? What are the effects on the other children? How do they feel?

Outside the family the range of risk areas is far greater for disabled children. Hospital care, respite, foster care, special buses and residential care are all potentially dangerous, and parents may be less likely to complain for fear of losing service, or because of complicated feelings about having a disabled child in the first place.

Russell (1994) writes about a mother who suspected a worker at a residential home which she used for occasional respite of physically abusing her child, but who had become part of the collusion that failed to bring this to light.

It is clearly the role of professional workers in all these fields to be alert to the possibility of abuse by their colleagues and to report their suspicions, if necessary by whistle blowing. While there are a raft of organisational issues involved here, professional workers have a role to play in influencing the conditions in which they work. They also have responsibilities as commissioners of service to ensure that children are not exposed to high risk situations by building as many safeguards into the contract as possible.

Professional associations are crucial in supporting members who may need to challenge the organisations in which they work, but they also concern themselves with setting standards for their members. This can be a double-edged sword. The professions of medicine and nursing have strict regulatory bodies which can discipline members and withdraw the right to practise. Yet doctors and nurses are accorded confidence by the public and by their colleagues as a result of their professional status and this can obscure serious and sometimes fatal abuse. Social workers will soon be subject to professional regulation by a new General Social Care Council, although at the time of writing it is proposed that such registration will be on a voluntary basis. The onus will therefore be on employers to choose whether to use registered staff.

Good practitioners/good practice

As a counter to the negative images portrayed earlier in the chapter, this section makes use of the evidence from the students and from other research with children and parents to describe the sort of people and actions which could ensure more helpful professionals. This description should not intimidate practitioners who may not meet these ideals. It is intended to offer some suggestions about the kind of issues which those managing services could usefully address and some ingredients which inter-professional training might provide.

Working with disabled children needs an understanding of health, welfare, education, child development, family functioning, law and disability rights as well as skills in counselling, listening, advocacy and an understanding of anti-discriminatory practice. Whatever their particular backgrounds, effective workers will need competence in a wide range of areas that are unlikely to be provided as a coherent body of knowledge on any particular professional training course.

Working with disabled children is still usually an 'extra' for healthcare workers, teachers, doctors and social workers. This represents a fundamental failure to recognise that key skills such as different ways to communicate and anti-discriminatory practice are applicable to all children.

Good professionals need an understanding of the interface between the organisation for which they work, and the service users to whom they are responsible. This is not solely their own responsibility. Increasing pressure by some organisations for professional staff to put organisational objectives ahead of professional considerations has been noted in many fields, but the time has passed when professional judgement can exclude an appreciation of resource implications and organisational priorities. The professional who can understand the need to ration, and how the budget works, will be in a better position to influence the way it operates than one who refuses to acknowledge the reality of limited resources. This does not deny the professional's responsibility to advocate for a specific client group, even in the face of organisational and peer group pressure, but it suggests that negotiation from a basis of understanding is more productive. Nor does understanding the reality of resource limitation mean that professionals have to accept it without question. However, arguing for increased resources is likely to be fairer to the client group as a whole if such representation is undertaken on a collective basis.

As well as understanding their own organisations, professionals need to feel comfortable working in the multi disciplinary arena, respecting and understanding the contributions of others. Professional boundaries in community care are likely to become increasingly blurred, and it is more important to start with a picture of what the child and family needs and how to provide it, than it is to continue arguments about which professional can best do what. It follows from much of what I have discussed earlier that putting children first, listening to their concerns and getting to know them lies at the heart of good practice. This means identifying and then finding ways to remove the barriers to their ambitions, and where this is not possible, to explain why and to seek viable alternatives. This requires a wide knowledge of available services, the imagination to develop new ones, and the negotiating skills to make things happen.

It will not always be possible. Professional integrity means being honest with children about what can and cannot be achieved. It means simple things like not making promises which cannot be kept. It is extremely unkind to lead a child to believe a relationship is permanent when it will be time- or task-limited. More seriously, professionals need to avoid making false promises to make themselves feel more comfortable or to secure information. It is wholly unreasonable to promise to remove an abuser knowing it may be beyond one's power to do so. Trust is fragile. Professionals need to learn to be open and truthful, especially about what might hurt.

Professional helpers have to learn not to dismiss the concerns of children, however trivial they may seem or however awkwardly expressed. With disabled children, there is a need to be familiar with a range of means to communicate, both verbally and non-verbally, or failing that, to know how to get in touch with suitable facilitators, interpreters and Human Aids to Communication where necessary.

In a rationed service, professionals need to prioritise their time, which means limiting the effort spent in determining a child's eligibility for services. Poor procedures can draw time away, or provide excuses for not moving forward. They can sound benign, but must be recognised for what they are. 'Sensitive' and 'need more information' may be codes for going slowly and failing to reach decisions.

Good practice: including the child in assessment

I heard a great deal from disabled students, social workers and from community nurses while writing this book about the amount of time and energy now devoted to feeding the cuckoo of assessment. I may have attracted this acrimony, having written a guidebook on the subject, but even allowing for that it is clear that assessment is widely regarded as over-emphasised, over done, time consuming and, worst of all, producing no effective guide to action. Yet it is the key to good practice. Good assessment does not stop with a plan which may lie unregarded on a shelf but includes negotiating, securing services and monitoring outcomes. If continual assessment has become a substitute for service provision then those professionals involved need to blow a collective whistle.

Social work assessments, if they are to enhance the self worth of the child, need to have their purpose clearly understood by all the workers involved. They must be explained to, and agreed with, the child. Crucially they should be understood as an assessment of a situation, or an evaluation of a proposed or current course of action rather than being understood as an assessment of the child herself. The last will always seem like a test, with possibilities for pass or failure. If this essential purpose is clear, *the child becomes an essential part of the assessment team*, and contributes to the judgements it is making, rather than being the subject of the exercise.

It is therefore not the child who will succeed or fail, or be judged, but *the plan* which is made as the result of the assessment process. This distinction is crucial to how the child experiences the assessment, and to attaining or maintaining self respect and a sense of control of the process.

It does not mean the child can choose any path he or she likes: life is more complicated than that, nor should responsibility be abdicated by parents and professionals. Rather the child is in a position to evaluate different options with the help of the assessment team; to help prioritise those issues or difficulties that should be tackled first; and to work out how to review the progress of the plan. Nor does it mean assessment is a voluntary exercise. Children may find themselves involved in assessments because schools, medical staff, parents or others request it, but it is foolish to expect that an assessment will have much meaning unless the child is willing to co-operate with it. The most likely way to engage children's co-operation is by ensuring that they are part of the assessment team. As far as age and understanding allow, they must be included in discussions about how, where, why, and with whom recorded material is shared.

It follows from this that the first stage of the assessment process proper is to ascertain the wishes of the child. Before that, however, there is usually much preliminary work to be done in establishing a working relationship, and a means of communication. Assessments vary, but they are logical processes and should follow more or less the process outlined in Appendix 3.

The trust of the child and family have to be earned. There will be a range of practical measures to be sorted out such as determining the means of communication, the timing and place of the assessment, and who will be involved in it. These are not separate issues. If the means of sorting out these practical measures is helpful, and involves the child, then the preliminary task of gaining trust will be all the easier. Establishing groundrules, and sticking to them, is one way of working this out.

Effective communication lies at the heart of any relationship and is crucial to assessment. Some disabled children need or prefer to communicate by means other than speech. Many children like tapping into computers, drawing and constructing charts. Computers can give voice to children who might shrink from talking to strangers. It is worthwhile spending time establishing the best ways of communicating and bearing in mind it may involve more than one method, such as asking questions verbally and getting the answers by computer screen. If the social worker is lucky the child will already have a means of communication, which is tried, tested and practised. Fostering communication skills is not something which should wait for assessment but should form part of the child's day-to-day development. If this has not occurred, then working out how the child might best communicate and trying out different things will have to run alongside the assessment.

If the assessment occurs after some trauma this may not be quite as enjoyable as it should be since pressure to make contact under such circumstances can be stressful for both parties. The child needs to understand that the social worker is prepared to persist, but not carry out an insistent interrogation which borders on harassment. On the other hand, workers should be aware that children like to play, and observing an inexperienced professional trying to communicate can provide hours of happy diversion.

Children may like to keep their own files, or record the assessment in other ways, such as on audio tape or video. This can include copies of reports, photographs or plans of action. Alternatively it could be separate records compiled by the child. These activities may be new to the child, and showing them diaries or tapes made by other children (with their agreement), may be helpful. Getting them to talk to other children with whom the social worker has worked may also be worth considering.

The crucial point is that the child feels a part of the assessment team, and that the assessment is something that is being worked on together. Assessments may not simply be routine procedures to work out future plans, but may relate to particular problems raised, perhaps by teachers, parents or healthcare staff. Time spent unravelling these enables the situation to be understood from the child's perspective. This means exploring the issues that arise from the disabling condition itself, but also broadening this to look at difficulties that arise because of environmental barriers, people's attitudes or poor service provision. The child will probably be more familiar with answering questions about what he or she can and cannot do than addressing issues about the difficulties that others cause, or what might help.

There has been a great deal of tension in recent years between the medical model, which holds that the existence of an impairment is in itself an explanation for the individual's failure to achieve a reasonable quality of life, and the social model, which shifts this emphasis away from pathologising the individual and talks of restricting environments and attitudes. In attempting to redress the balance away from the former medical agenda, some exponents of the social model have adopted positions which deny there are any difficulties arising from the impairment itself, and as such no necessity to consider change or cure.

This reflects thinking from groups such as the anti-racism and Gay Pride movements, and has much to recommend it as an affirmation of the equal value of all people regardless of difference, but it is arguable that the uncompromising nature of the perspective has created resistance in some professional circles to accepting the social model. It is important to seek a balanced perspective and acknowledge that difficulties may arise from the impairment itself as well as recognising that the ways in which children with impairments experience their lives are also dependent on other people's attitudes and behaviours.

The assessment model which I would suggest is therefore one which starts with the aspirations, hopes and ambitions of the child, as well as those of their parents, and then works out how these can be realised both by identifying positive routes forward, and by identifying barriers. Social workers do not have magic wands and need to be honest about what they can and cannot achieve, while giving the child faith that they are committed to working on the problems together. An important lesson from the social model is to develop in the child a clear understanding that problems can lie in their environment and education. It is not their fault. This does not mean that there is nothing children can do to help themselves, but recognises that dealing with disablement is not an individual struggle but a collective one. How this is all explained will depend on the age and understanding of the child, but the essential message is that having an impairment does not mean they are 'bad', nor are they responsible for 'overcoming' it.

If ascertaining the wishes and hopes of the child proves difficult, either because of intellectual development, or because the child has come to believe that they are not expected to have views and have no conception of how to formulate them, then an alternative must be sought. Siblings may be useful here, and in any case should always be considered as potentially important partners in the assessment team. Another possibility is for the social worker to make suggestions, on the basis of 'other children have found' or simply 'have you thought about?'. These may start with the activities that are common for a child of the same gender and age, living in the same area, and then working out what needs to be put into place to enable the disabled child to engage in the same or similar activities. This may not reflect what the parents would prefer, but if other teenage children spend Saturday afternoons hanging out at MacDonalds then disabled young people will get on better with their peers by doing the same thing. This can be conceptualised as an end in itself, or as part of a grander plan toward social integration, confidence building or independence.

Barriers to achieving this end have to be surmounted. They may be practical, such as transport, finance, the right clothes to wear, or attitudes of the family or other young people. Breaking the process down into steps is usually helpful and makes what initially seem like impossible ambitions more manageable. It is also important to let children try things, even if they fail. People rarely regret things they do, looking back, but frequently regret those that they never had the chance to try. Children need to explore and work out their own limitations.

The social worker can help by noting how children cope with difficulties, and what sort of things they use to deal with disappointment, anxiety or problems. If these are helpful they can be encouraged and extended into other areas of life so that children learn that they have resources and skills which are transferable and will continue to serve them. Involving the child means paying due attention to his or her concerns, however trivial, and recording these in the same way as what may seem to be larger issues. There is room for negotiation here, given that the adults in the team may have differing priorities from the child or siblings. A suggestion that 'we'll try this out, if you'll try the other' might prove more attractive than, for example, 'do this because we say so'.

Once aspirations are worked out and prioritised, identifying options for meeting them is the next logical stage. Possibilities need to be explored, either verbally or experientially. Plans should be open and displayed, but only as possibilities, not blueprints. Plans are there to be changed if necessary, and children should be reminded that if there is a change of plan because something does not work out, it is the plan that is the problem, not them. It may need redrawing, or tweaking, or it may be that some vital ingredient or piece of work has been missed out. It may be that some more data is needed, or further advice.

This model of assessment is a single example of how an intervention could look if planned with the child's best interests at heart. The aim of professional intervention is to identify and provide solutions to the child's problems, whether they result directly from an impairment, or from the kind of structural, environmental and attitudinal barriers described earlier (Swain *et al.*, 1998). Intervention should not be designed simply to solve problems caused by the child and identified by others. The difference is crucial, and its application as a thinking tool to all proposed professional interventions would facilitate a fundamental shift from disabling to enabling provision.

Conclusion

I have written this chapter in the belief that professionals working with children need not and should not start from a different point when the children are disabled. Sound welfare, medical and educational principles, ethics and practices still apply. The challenge is to ensure these are extended to include and take account of children who are physically different from the majority. That much professional practice has become a special enterprise does not reflect children's needs but the fears and prejudices about disability that have permeated society. Professionals should reaffirm confidence in their skills and knowledge and incorporate an awareness of the discriminatory forces which can make them react in contradiction of sound principles.

Neither professionals nor their organisations will achieve this SEAchange single-handedly, but it represents a goal towards which both can work. This is not to pretend it will be easy. So long as disabled children are perceived as an insignificant part of the human race, or even as creatures beyond it, it will be easier to expect them to adjust to fit it, rather than expecting any change in the rest of society. When we learn to understand that the way we treat disabled children affects and reflects the whole of our behaviour and interactions with each other as a society, we can make that fundamental shift to include rather than exclude.

Chapter 5

Organisational Change

'High needs for medical or nursing care are not a reason for failing to meet the ordinary needs of people for a good quality of life. High healthcare needs can be met in non-institutional settings if the issues relating to staff competence and skills are addressed.'

(Signposts for Success, NHS Executive, 1998, p 68)

'The introduction of Best Value represents the biggest challenge to local government since the introduction of compulsory competitive tendering in the 1980s.'

(Audit Commission, 1998)

'An inclusive ethos would, by definition, stress the need for sympathetic and positive responses to anyone with any sort of difficulties or difference.'

(Lewis, 1995, p 169)

Introduction

A successful service organisation will have to value both its service users and the staff who provide the service. In addition, where public money is concerned, it must satisfy increasingly stringent criteria in demonstrating that it is making best use of public money. The Audit Commission (1998) states that this means going 'back to basics and examining fundamental objectives and priorities' (p 4). This chapter is based on the assumption that the principle of social inclusion provides a common goal which can be shared with service users, professional staff and central government.

Successfully changing an organisation means having a vision of its purpose and future development which takes account of competing influences, such as current practice, resources, government direction, new thinking and the consumer's views. In practical terms, both structural and attitudinal change may be needed. This chapter is divided into two sections: it starts by discussing users' views, before discussing how organisational cultures or value bases might be addressed. In the second part, it focuses more specifically on change in two arenas: first, community services, which takes health and social services together in line with current thinking, and second education. In each case the underlying ethos is to move toward service provision which does not discriminate on the basis of physical difference.

Section I: Value-based organisations

Consulting service users

A conversation from the American television drama *ER* highlights the dilemma of service providers. One of the doctors in the Emergency Room, which in the UK would be called an Accident and Emergency Unit, is complaining after a difficult shift that 'we can't help people who can't help themselves'. The nurse responds to him that he is wrong: 'Those are exactly the people we should be helping.' ('When the bough breaks', broadcast in the UK 28th January 1998.)

This highlights the question: who are health and social welfare organisations for, and on what basis? Many service users encountering them may be forgiven for thinking that they are not designed to encourage their custom! For example, Gardner found reception areas in some social services to be ill lit, poorly decorated, infrequently cleaned and uncomfortable (Gardner, 1998). In their study of access for disabled people, Swain and his colleagues found that much information in social services offices was out of date in respect of service location, and that staff were unaware of disability issues. They cite the experience of service users who had to telephone five or six numbers before getting the information they wanted, and the lack of easy availability of material in Braille or on audio tape (Swain *et al.*, 1998).

Health centres and GP surgeries have done a great deal to improve physical conditions but the trend toward centralised services in the health service is cresting other access difficulties. Many local hospitals are closing to rationalise complex specialities on fewer sites, typically out of city centres. These specialities have come to include accident and emergency services. These rationalisations may work in terms of concentrating professional expertise, but greater travel distances present difficulties both for patients and for their visitors, especially those who rely on public transport. Parents with children in tow, disabled or otherwise, may find that simply making the journey to hospital has exhausted them.

Taking due note of consumer views could help organisations become more user friendly. Positive changes include such things as accessible buildings, readily available information, talking to people as equal partners, keeping appointments on time and keeping promises.

Consultation is less easy when the group in question are children.

This is not an excuse for not making the effort. There are a number of methods which would give disabled children more of a voice.

(1) Consulting directly with disabled children who are users of services.
(2) Research with disabled adults who have used services in the past.
(3) Consultation with parents as advocates for their children.
(4) Using disabled adults both as advocates and as members of staff.
(5) Independent evaluation.

Consulting children directly

In the UK the Social Services Inspectorate have set standards for service for 'disabled children and their families' which include consultation with children. There are 12 such standards derived from the Children Act (England and Wales) 1989 against each of which are a number of criteria for measurement. Meeting the SSI Standards for disabled as well as non-disabled children ought to be a reasonable aim for local authorities, and yet the SSI found that most standards were not being met where disabled children were concerned (SSI/DoH, 1994). For example, Standard 3 asks that 'the child's wishes and feelings have been sought in considering decisions which are likely to affect their daily life or their future' (Guidance to the Children Act Volume 6, para 6.6–6.9). The SSI found that staff in local authorities did not have the requisite skills to consult children directly; nor did they find any evidence of advocacy schemes in the authorities inspected (SSI/DoH, 1994).

There are two main options here, and organisations can make use of both. One is an ongoing dialogue with children who are consumers of their particular service. The second is to make use of independent research findings which report direct conversations with disabled children who are service users of similar organisations. Both are comparatively recent developments for researchers in welfare (as opposed to education), but there are a growing number of studies recently published or in progress which are involving disabled children in the research. (For example, Edinburgh and Leeds Universities and The Ann Craft Trust all have studies in progress, as has independent researcher Jenny Morris.) As well as conducting interviews, Leeds University produces a newsletter which invites contributions from 11–16-year-old disabled children about their family, friends, attitudes, school, going out, hospitals and getting involved. Children can write, ring, use an e-mail address or ask the research team to visit.

There are limitations to such consultation, in that children cannot be expected to take full responsibility for their own health, welfare or education. However, the idea that adulthood is a settled state, whereas childhood is transitory, leads to childhood being conceived of as incomplete or inferior, so that children are less likely to be consulted since the adult must, by definition, know best. There is a balance to be struck between ensuring that children benefit from adult experience, while not denying the value of their own.

Daunt asks adults to recognise that in addition to education, the quality of life for children 'needs to be made up of components which reflect their actual needs and desires during childhood itself' (Daunt, 1996).

Adult-led models, however child-centred, cannot substitute for open discussions with children which reflect their priorities, which may reflect either present needs or their concerns for the future. Seeking this kind of openness is of course fraught with all kind of methodological difficulties, not the least of which is that children are not used to being asked, but these are essentially practical problems which the enthusiastic researcher should relish. Interviewing children is a skill requiring sufficient understanding of child development to ask appropriate questions, and to pose them in the right way. There is useful literature in this area, mainly developing from work with abused children (for example, Bannister *et al.*, 1997; Roberts & Taylor, 1993).

Listening to children may mean that the adult hears things that are uncomfortable. Butler (1998) found that children believed adults to be insincere. They did not distinguish between parents and professional helpers such as teachers in this. Adults were thought to either trivialise and belittle children's experiences, or totally overreact. The latter tended to rebound on the children themselves. Adults were also thought to gossip too much. This matches the retrospective views of the students, where a number of the adults about whom they talked had been more concerned with their own performance and image than with the needs of the children.

Children need adults who make them feel safe, not just in the physical sense, but also in the sense of psychological security. Adults need to be trustworthy, not to act without consulting the child and thus to allow them a measure of self determination. This includes adults respecting and keeping confidences and not allowing their own needs and fears to dominate the relationship.The Utting report (1997) included a list of pointers from children themselves, which merit serious discussion:

> Employ the right kind of staff
> > with a good sense of humour
> > with a good attitude towards children
> > who try to understand children
> > who do not shout at children
> > who have been closely vetted.

> Allow children and young people to have a range of positive experiences.

> Give them a choice about which adults to approach for support.

Help them become independent and confident.

Develop a culture of openness.

Make sure all, especially the younger ones, know what their rights are.

Ensure there is a difference in atmosphere between school and home.

Ensure that people of all ages can mix – do not separate older and younger children.

Be protective and look after them.

Install security cameras.

Install security alarms.

Employ security guards.

(Utting, 1997, p 84)

While these recommendations derive from an investigation into how children in residential settings could be protected from abuse, and reflect views of children who felt unsafe, they are useful indicators for any organisation wishing to be more responsive to children. Addressing the concerns behind these suggestions and giving them serious attention in planning services would go well beyond keeping children safe and forming the basis of a child centred service.

Retrospective research

Retrospective research, such as that used in this book, means listening to adults, or older children, and asking them to reflect on their childhood experiences. The advantages of this method are that respondents have had time to consider and reflect on their situations, and should not feel pressurised to give the 'right answers' which may affect children currently in receipt of services. There are fewer problems in obtaining meaningful consent than are involved in talking to children. Adults can review the whole of their childhood, and assess situations and services more generally.

Such research carries the disadvantage of always relating to past situations. Those making use of their comments have to assess any possible changes in service provision which have occurred since the respondents were young. Nevertheless, this kind of data is rare enough to be highly valuable to organisations who wish to listen, and provides a number of key messages which indicate that children's priorities do not necessarily match those of their parents. It is also powerful data in that it comes from adults who have had the experience of being disabled as children, the time to reflect on its meaning and the advantage of setting it in context of their childhood. It cannot be dismissed by reluctant service providers as only representing a child's current perception, interpretation of events or level of understanding.

Consultation with parents as advocates for their children

Most research involving parents has focused on their needs, but they are also the main advocates for disabled children, in a society where legislation on a child's behalf is poorly enforced unless there is pressure from individuals or organisations. Their input is therefore an essential ingredient in any organisational changes. A great deal has been written about 'partnership' since the Children Act 1989 and the Education Acts 1981 and 1993 (all England and Wales) cast parents as partners of service providers, but in reality there is much reluctance on both sides. Of course parents and service providers are not exclusive groups; professional workers may have children who are disabled. Beresford's research with parents of disabled children included some indications of what they believed their children needed (Beresford, 1995). Over $\frac{3}{4}$ thought their children had unmet needs. These included help in developing social and relationship skills and opportunities to meet other children, both disabled and non-disabled, as well as someone to talk to about being disabled. Beresford concluded that much attention has been focused on the cognitive and motor development of disabled children and too little on their social lives, 'despite the fact that inter-action with peers is well recognised as an important influence on children's development and well being' (p 84).

There are a number of pitfalls inherent in direct consultation with parents, as opposed to making use of research. Many parents do not have time to act as representatives, a role which entails a two-way dialogue between the organisation and a constituency of other parents. Those who do attend meetings can normally be seen as a parent 'voice' rather than representative. This role is at once less pressured and less powerful, but such a construction more easily leaves the door open for other voices to be heard. Only in schools is it usually possible to get groups of parents together. Other agencies more commonly rely on fewer individuals, and some often acquire a single willing parent, who may turn up at any number of different locations. Such an individual can be extremely helpful in framing policies, but can easily become an alibi for not seeking a wider perspective. Another difficulty for parents is the fear that they may jeopardise their children's position if they 'protest too much'. Opportunities have to be provided for people to indicate what is helpful or unhelpful on a routine basis so that commenting on provision feels normal.

Another obvious way around this is to involve parents early or in planning new services, so that they are not criticising existing ones. This may seem idealistic, but the introduction of new legislation is offering agencies ample opportunities to go back to the drawing board. Both Education and Health Action Zones started to emerge in 1998, and Primary Care Groups take on some new responsibilities in 1999.

Using disabled adults both as advocates and as members of staff

It is useful for organisations which wish to work in the interests of disabled children to consider ways of bringing more disabled adults into visible positions. This is not to assume that adults can act as proxies for disabled children, or that services which are appropriate for adults will work, but disabled children receive poor service because of their disability as well as because of their minority. Disabled adults are in a good position to challenge that and to recognise when discriminatory assumptions are being made. Disabled children may not encounter many or any disabled adults and may entertain unhelpful assumptions about them, and about their own futures, as a result.

I was very struck by the comments made by a respondent in the Preston survey about the first time she had encountered an adult with cerebral palsy, and the surprise that created:

> 'When I was ten or eleven I went to the Spastics Society's headquarters to have psychological profiles and things and there were disabled adults there, and that was the first time that I had seen a disabled adult. It made me realise I would grow up.'

This reminded me of the need I felt as a social worker to prepare children and parents in advance for the encounters they would have with disabled adults when I took them to the Spastics Society's (now SCOPE) assessment centre in Fitzroy Square in London. Their previous lack of contact with any disabled adults meant the adjustment to their thinking about their own future was sudden. This could be reassuring or frightening depending on the particular individuals they met. More than one disabled child with whom I worked had believed that they would walk normally when they grew up, simply because all the adults they had encountered could walk. It could be a shock for parents too: seeing for the first time how their own baby might grow up. In clinics and assessment centres, parents are more likely, of course, to encounter disabled adults who are ill or in difficulties, perhaps gaining an unbalanced impression of disabled living. Increased visibility of disabled adults in all walks of life would make these sudden adjustments to thinking unnecessary. On a more structured basis, mentoring schemes using disabled adults would be valuable means of support for disabled children as well as providing a route to feed information to the organisation about difficulties in the system.

Independent evaluation

For a range of reasons service users or staff who are asked for their views directly may be less than forthright. Organisations seeking to inform themselves of the quality and appropriateness of their service provision could commission independent research. There are many independent contractors who will undertake such surveys, as will many university departments. As with any important purchase, the buyer is advised to take a number of precautions to ensure value for money, but research is more than a purchase. If it is to be of real value, it is a partnership between the organisation, the research team and the service users.

This will mean devoting time to finding the right team to commission, plan and agree goals and objectives, and allocating a senior member of staff both to negotiate with the researchers, and to facilitate their access to appropriate staff and service users. These latter groups need to be involved as early as possible if they are to be committed to the research, and to the implementation of its recommendations.

Valuing staff

As I have argued earlier, a successful service organisation will have to value both its service users and the staff who provide the service. These aims are intertwined. Sadly, the current position is that disabled children, and those who work directly with them on a day-to-day basis, occupy low status positions in society. Finding ways of making people feel good about themselves means valuing and recognising contributions throughout people's childhood and adult lives, in a way which is quite different from the current pattern where so many children fail or fall short. Allowing more children to be successful does not mean making examinations easier to pass, but involves broadening criteria for success. For example, in describing links between children with learning disability and groups of non-disabled children, Lewis notes that the former group's ability to use Makaton sign language not only gave them a skill which helped their confidence in relation to the 'cleverer' children, but gave them something to share with them (Lewis, 1995).

This way forward involves a major shift in thinking which runs counter to current trends where league tables, performance indicators and constant measurement of achievement are becoming embedded in the educational system. Such trends individualise academic achievement. They set less value on interpersonal achievements such as sociability, respect for others, co-operation, helpfulness or leadership. All these are harder to measure. This is somewhat ironic since they are qualities which are valued by employers and often sought after in job selection. This is not to suggest that a disabled child is any better or any worse in these areas than a non-disabled child, but to widen the scope of what is valued and rewarded at school and in the rest of life might enable more children to be successful in the short term, and fit them to be better citizens in the long term. This would benefit all children who currently fail to get to the top of the class or make it into the team.

Enabling more people to feel good about themselves may also reduce the kind of unhelpful behaviour perpetrated on others by those who have low self esteem, and who feel undervalued in the work that they do. For example, much quality control in service industries depends on complaints or grievance systems. This negative feedback only recognises what is going wrong and can result in a 'watch-your-back' or 'it's not my job' culture. Organisations need to find ways to recognise and reward actions and behaviours which enhance their operation in a positive way. Many hotels now operate 'employee of the month' competitions based on feedback from guests about employees who have been particularly helpful. Selected employees' photographs are displayed as a result.

Consulting children about teaching assistants, care staff or social workers who have been helpful may be useful in that it gives children some power as well as publicly recognising the kind of behaviours that please them. These may well be different from the performance indicators used by management appraisal schemes, and thus widen the scope of what is rewarded. While such schemes may be flawed, for example in that the person who cleans out the toilets is less likely to get noticed, they have the attraction of rewarding actions which may not necessarily require high levels of skill nor a senior position in the organisation but which matter to the consumer. They also recognise the value of positive attitudes toward service users.

Beyond that, employers have to find ways to enable front line staff to do their work in a way which is not subservient. They can then maintain self esteem without resorting to belittling or abusing the service users. This is an attitudinal issue. It means reaching a relationship with service users based on mutuality of respect and a recognition that *both* parties have a right to dignity, choice and to be treated with politeness. Empowering service users does not give them the right to mis-use staff. This may cause particular problems with some male service users and young women staff, but it is an attitudinal issue which applies across the board.

Underpinning and exaggerating insensitive behaviours towards disabled children may be the mistaken beliefs that such children do not feel pain or that they will not notice whether they are fed clumsily or not. Even if the impairment itself is permanent, there may be room for improvement either on a day-to-day basis in how the child experiences events and activities, or in the longer term in the sense of acquiring new and better ways of managing things and situations. It is not wise to exclude basic grade staff from policy making discussions or consultations about practice. Making time to discuss better ways of working as a staff group, and sharing good ideas, not only helps to spread good practice, but helps the employees to feel their contribution matters and that the management want to listen. These discussions can be semi-formal and the outcomes recorded to give the contributions a recognised value. Such actions also counter the informal culture in which bad practice can spread because the more powerful individuals in the staff are left to control what happens on a day-to-day basis.

There has been disagreement about the value of antidiscrimination statements by organisations in terms of race or gender: both arenas in which discrimination is against the law. Such statements in themselves serve little purpose unless they are backed up by appropriate policies and procedures which are well followed up, and understood by staff. However, despite these obvious limitations, it is reasonable for an organisation to start by making a public commitment to change. The very fact of announcing change, or setting new institutional standards, may at least put issues on the agenda and open them up for debate and discussion. It offers a benchmark against which individuals can measure themselves and each other, and which can be invoked when changes in practice are advocated. The fact that an organisation states openly that it will not tolerate racist language from its staff sets a baseline standard and clarifies the expected quality of behaviour. Similar statements about how staff address and talk about disabled children in their care are a useful indicator about expectations in schools or residential care.

Such statements can also empower managers to insist that staff adhere to standards, whether or not the staff in question are personally convinced of their value. Changing behaviour rather than attitudes is a contentious issue, and staff may themselves invoke their own 'freedom' to resist the imposition of standards of behaviour or use of language. From the perspective of the minority group member, one argument is that it is preferable to have hostility out in the open so that at least the enemy is visible. Black footballer John Barnes commented on proposals to make the use of racist language by football fans an offence at matches:

> 'What happens is racist fans can just keep their mouths shut for 90 minutes and then continue their racist behaviour the rest of the week. The fact that they're quiet doesn't mean we're getting rid of racism. In many respects, its driving it underground.'

> (*Guardian*, 10th December 1997)

The counterview is that it is preferable to be free from assaults or insults, whether this is attained through voluntary compliance or is imposed, in much the same way that the police are expected to protect citizens from crime rather than seek to convince potential criminals to desist by force of reason.

If organisations set clear standards in terms of how staff relate to each other and to clients, they can attempt to convince those staff who need to change that these are appropriate behaviours, but without in any way making their compliance an option. This may mean some staff will leave, and others may bury their prejudices while at work, but it ensures organisational expectations are clear and sends a very important message to the minority group concerned that discrimination against them is not tolerated. This latter message is just as vital to organisational health as the one to the potential oppressor.

What kind of standards?

The use of language which diminishes, demeans, mocks or excludes can be actively discouraged. Disabled children may not be in a position to counter such language themselves, nor is it appropriate that a child should have to, so it is important that staff take such responsibility on themselves. This means openly discussing what sort of language is acceptable, and what may be hurtful. This is more helpful than issuing manuals of correct or incorrect speech for two reasons.

First, the discussion itself is important and helps involve staff in the process. Imposition of the details of standards from above is the final resort, not the first stage. What could be set from above is the organisational objective, for example 'not to diminish disabled children'.

Second, language is dynamic and manuals go quickly out of date. Words and phrases which were once quite acceptable become unacceptable, while others are sanitised with time. Additionally, as groups become more self confident they can become less sensitive and words and phrases which seemed stigmatic become rehabilitated. Words such as 'old', 'queer' and 'deaf' have undergone this process, as members of those groups become less worried about identifying with the label and more concerned with the rights of the group concerned.

Children could be included in conversations which take place in their sight or hearing. This may simply mean explaining or rephrasing, but it may mean translating. Children who cannot see could be told what is happening. Staff can use children's own names, rather than nicknames or generalisations, unless the children specifically request otherwise. When addressing each other, staff could use names consistently. Calling some staff by first names, and others by title or rank, creates needless hierarchies which diminish the value of those at the bottom.

In general, staff could set an example to children by the way in which they interact with each other. If management is seen to diminish the status of care staff or teaching assistants this not only undermines their self respect but also reflects on the value of the children they work with. Staff who are 'good with children' should be valued by the organisation, and not accorded low status. Interaction between staff may also involve friendship and sexual relationships. These can provide children with valuable role models.

Children's cultural identities need sensitive handling. This may not be as simple as ensuring appropriate dress, food and religious observations, although all are important. Many children in care are caught between cultures and may not be best helped by staff who insist they ritualistically observe their own culture in isolation from the rest of the children. A child who was forced against her wishes to eat halal food and dress differently from her friends caused me considerable consternation as a social worker. It is a question of finding a reasonable balance which does not cut some children off from their generation in the name of their religion or cultural heritage, nor cut them off from their culture because of their minority status.

This is not easy to achieve, especially with disabled children who are already in danger of becoming isolated from their contemporaries by their physical difference. Culture is something which is lived *with* others, not derived from books. This reinforces the importance wherever possible of same race, same religion placements in school, foster care and residential care as well as the availability of black and Asian staff and mentors. Achieving balance means recognising the importance for all children of friendships and interactions across cultural and racial differences, which involves enjoying each others traditions. It also means recognising that children and young people may have different priorities and concerns from adults, and that disabled children have as much right to rebel as non-disabled youngsters, and to face the same consequences!

Organisations could review their dress codes. Staff who work directly with children need not dress down, nor is it necessary to don protective clothing to feed children. In my experience putting on an apron or overall before feeding a child is more likely to result in the staff member being careless and spilling food or even looking elsewhere and causing injuries. Staff could engage with children directly and especially when feeding, dressing or washing. It is an organisational issue to ensure there is adequate time for this.

Children could have some choice about which staff work with them, especially in personal areas such as feeding, dressing and personal hygiene. They could also be allowed to choose who to confide in. Just as staff could be included in discussions about how the organisation runs, so too could the children. There are various ways of doing this even with children who are less naturally forthcoming, such as setting aside time during each day for group discussion or feedback (see for example, Lewis, 1995, Moseley, 1994).

Sexual harassment should be taken seriously, whether this is between staff and other staff, by staff towards children in their care, by residents to staff or between children and young people themselves. Utting (1997) points out that sexual feeling can be especially charged in residential settings and advises on the importance of protocols in relation to sex, taking account of both heterosexual and homosexual feelings (p 115).

Despite this entirely reasonable and sensible advice, much sexual harassment does not reflect healthy sexual attraction. Rather it is a mechanism for abusing power, and as readily as any other form of abuse it should attract censure and disciplinary action, including dismissal and criminal proceedings.

A commitment by an organisation to a social model would involve focusing on the child's environment, and thinking in terms of removing barriers to their aspirations. This is a completely different approach from simply exhorting a child to do better, in that it recognises the role that external forces play in encouraging or hindering wellbeing and development.

Finally, organisations have to demonstrate that they value their consumers by treating them as partners, and openly sharing information with them, even when it is unpalatable. The imperative to be open could make systems fairer. For example, rationing may be a necessary feature in an organisation where demand outstrips supply, but it is important that crude rationing devices are replaced by those which can be justified as having some rational and fair basis. The Audit Commission's concept of Best Value is that councils should be responsible to the people 'who pay for and use their services' (Audit Commission 1998, p 4). Rationing devices may be presented as being in the public interest, but it is important to remember that 'service users' and 'the public' who are footing the bill are not two distinct groups.

Swain and his colleagues argue that the social support required by disabled people is regarded by the local authority as 'special needs' rather than civil rights, and that systems which prioritise need deny many disabled people the resources required to live an ordinary life (Swain *et al.*, 1998). Parents of disabled children need to feel that their concerns are taken seriously and are not abnormal. For their sake, and that of the child, they should not have to 'fight' or beg for service, nor have to present their cases as abnormal in order to secure help.

Section II: The seamless service

Community care: health and social services working together

Health and welfare are provided within a changing context. Lately there has been a political drive to dissolve the boundaries between them. There is ministerial concern about the 'faultlines that have developed in service provision between social services and health authorities, around specific themes, one of which is children's services' (Boateng, 1997). Children who are different from the majority do not fall neatly into anyone's services. Like all children they will make demands at some time during their lives on education, welfare and health services, some of which will be considerable. Because of their difference, they will find themselves at the heart of the multidisciplinary enterprise, yet on the fringes of each individual agency's priorities or central business. However, legally, they are 'in need' as long as they are children and disabled.

Children in need are defined by the Children Act (England and Wales) 1989 as

'(a) those unlikely to achieve or maintain, or have the opportunity of achieving or maintaining, a reasonable standard of health or development without the provision of services

(b) those whose health or development is likely to be significantly impaired, or further impaired, without the provision of such services

(c) those who are disabled.'

(S.17(10))

Those who framed the Act clearly did not think the first two categories broad enough to include disabled children who might benefit from services. Put another way, disabled children, even if they fall outside both of the first two definitions, are still deemed to be needy. This leaves no room for debate. What education, health and social services have argued over, therefore, is not the idea that disabled children are in need, but rather *which* children meet the definition of 'disabled' in relation to their particular service. The legal definition of disabled derives from the 1948 National Assistance Act:

'...a child is disabled if he is blind, deaf or dumb or suffers from mental disorder of any kind or is substantially and permanently handicapped by illness, injury or congenital deformity or any such disability as may be pre-scribed.'

(S.17(11)

Much of the above is a matter of opinion. The inclusion of the word 'substantial' in particular leaves considerable room for manoeuvre and inter-agency dispute.

Education and social services can find themselves arguing about the balance of budgetary responsibility for children cared for and educated away from home. The provision of services in the independent sector, as well as in local authorities and the various components of the health service, has created a complex array of resources each with its own assessment procedures, eligibility criteria, professional staff and cultures. Far from enhancing choice, increasing the number of services can be counterproductive, since each organisation takes a narrower slice of the same market rather than increasing the sum total of provision. I have written about this before in the context of the care continuum (Eley & Middleton, 1983). When a new service is introduced there are often the following consequences:

- more complicated selection procedures have to be introduced;
- there is increased pressure for those whose circumstances change to be provided for elsewhere;
- more gaps are created so that those who do not quite fit may fall through.

Since disabled children fall between the stools of health and social care, the proposed changes in the direction of multidisciplinary service, seamless service or GP co-ordinated care could help, provided that these children are included in the thinking of policy makers. This is far from being automatic: 'A Service with Ambitions', for example, makes no specific reference to disabled children: one must assume they are buried in the broad reference to 'people with special needs' (DoH, 1996, p 20).

'A Service with Ambitions' (DoH, 1996) outlines what were the last Conservative government's ambitions for the Health Service. It does not specifically refer to disabled children but the overall aims are relevant. Stephen Dorrell, then Secretary of State for Health, stated that the National Health Service had to work with other agencies and 'in particular it will only be possible to secure the fullest benefit from National Health Service resources against the background of close co-operation with social services' (DoH, 1996 p 5). Labour ministers have repeated the aim to ensure better working between health and social services.

Some of the key aims, in full below, give a flavour of the kind of service envisaged:

- 'As a matter of good practice, sharing relevant information is vital if multi-professional and inter-agency care is to function effectively. At the same time, people with special needs are entitled to the same confidential handling of information about their health or social care as any other patient' (p 20).
- 'Organisational and professional boundaries should be of no consequence to users and carers; multi-professional and multi-agency education, training and development can support this aim. It is vital that staff work closely with individuals and their families or carers' (p 20).
- 'The National Health Service and its partners should give increasing priority both to the prevention of physical and sensory disability, and to the problems associated with disability where it has been diagnosed. At the point of diagnosis people should be informed honestly, sensitively and fully of the nature and consequences of the disease and given access immediately to counselling, advice and support. The National Health Service should be leading the way in changing public attitudes towards disabled people' (p 21).

The Labour Government White Paper, 'The New National Health Service', issued in December 1997, reinforced the message that the National Health Service must work in partnership and promised to 'discard what has failed', which included fragmentation of services (DoH, 1997b).

Keeping pace with the implications of organisational change is difficult. The National Health Service is no longer one organisation but a

multitude of authorities, trusts, fundholders and independent contractors. Instead of simply struggling to understand social services they
now face internal struggles to understand each other and keep pace
with fundamental and persistant structural change. The situation is far
from settled. Trusts which proved too small are merging and Community Trusts are being replaced in the next few years by GP Primary
Care Trusts. For example, in one area, the Community Trust merged
with its neighbour during 1998, to cover a combined total of about
300,000 patients. This meant bringing together two management
structures and large staff groups. In three years time it faces further
upheaval, when its work will divide between three Primary Care Trusts
each serving around 100,000 patients. Purchasers wanting influence in
the market place are forming consortia. While the National Health
Service is facing up to the 'New National Health Service' (DoH 1997b),
local authorities are reviewing their services in the light of the 1998
White Paper, which contains proposals for more closely managed
childcare services, independent inspection including Children's Rights
Officers, and a new professional regulation body (DoH 1998).

Children's Service Plans are one method of formalising inter-agency
co-operation. Government made it mandatory for all local authorities
with social service functions to produce Children's Service Plans by
March 1997. These had previously had only the status of a recommendation from government (DoH/DFEE, 1997). Children's plans
needed to be multi-agency, and to describe services for which the
Authority had responsibility under part III of the Children Act 1989.
Their production was directed at social services because only they had
the necessary legal powers, but the 1997 White Paper noted that the
planning process should be corporate within the Local Authority and
fully involve other statutory services (DoH, 1997a). These plans across
the country have a great deal in common. Durham City's plan
'Managing the Future' is a fairly typical example (Durham Social Services, 1997).

According to their earlier and more modest consultation document,
called 'Investing in Children' Durham began the planning exercise by
'establishing shared values and principles across agency boundaries'.
This was followed by a series of agreed value statements, mainly based
on the 1989 United Nations Convention on the rights of the child. It did
not challenge the right of any agency to set its own resource priorities,
but only to 'secure the values and principles which would inform
individual agency and inter-agency planning' (Durham County
Council, 1996). This is reminiscent of both UN and European Commission documents which seek to establish broad principles rather than
determine individual State Law.

Typically these plans referred to 'children with disabilities' and
focused not on disabling environments, but on the children's or
families' difficulties. There is little evidence that the social model has

influenced the plans. Durham's Plan had four main aims: to finish the strategy in relation to disabled children, increase the range of services, demonstrate new partnerships with other agencies and record an increase in service user satisfaction. Only the first three were targeted as key aims in terms of performance monitoring.

The changes in both health and social services offer opportunities to do things differently, even within current resource constraints. Primary care groups will shift the balance of power from hospitals to community provision, and from Health Authorities to groups of general practitioners. As with any major change, there are threats and opportunities and a great many unpredictable factors. There are, for example, unproven assumptions within this thinking that community care is less expensive than hospital based care, and that general practitioners will prove to be better resource managers than those currently running services.

Those with an interest in developing higher quality services need to develop and retain a clear vision in terms of what is required in services for disabled children, and could seek to make appropriate representation to these new bodies. This could emphasise and encourage current good practice as well as reverse those practices which are disadvantageous. An aim to deliver healthcare on an equal basis to all children, according to their health needs, is preferable to one which separates some children on the basis of their physical or intellectual difference. For example, the Community Trust in my local area produces information for parents of all pre-school children which describes a wide range of services, including a child development centre, speech and physiotherapy. These are mingled with health promotion, dental health and chiropody. Nowhere in the leaflet are the terms disability or learning-disabled used, on the grounds that all the services may be needed by any child at some point. The Health Service Manager responsible told me she believed it important not to label young children as disabled, as it could result in their parents losing confidence in their abilities and developing an over reliance on external expertise. She advocated a low key approach both to parents and the extended family, which recognised that all children had developmental needs, and were not wholly predictable. Parents should not be encouraged to think that healthcare staff have all the answers.

A recognition that all children have the same needs means building from childcare principles. These may be culturally specific, but they should enable services to be developed around common goals and principles, whichever agency acts as the provider. For example, most people in the UK could probably agree that children are best raised at home with their own parents, within their own communities, that they should if possible be educated along with their peers, and that they should receive medical care when ill.

Starting from these childcare principles means finding ways within healthcare to support and give confidence to parents, carers, teachers, and others who work and care for children on a day-to-day basis. This runs counter to current arrangements whereby, if the child is diagnosed as 'disabled' or having 'special needs', parents and teachers can easily find themselves disempowered. One general practitioner, although aware that all children on his patch are his responsibility, described disabled children to me as an area he did not 'need to bother about'. While he welcomed the proposed new arrangements for Primary Care Trusts which would give him the power to allocate resources, he was less enthusiastic about the prospect of dealing directly with angry patients to whom he, and not some 'faceless bureaucrat', was denying treatment. General practitioners may need advice about ways to manage and support children, preferably in ways which maintain their families as carers and do not demand high cost alternatives. Hospitals may be comfortable environments for the hospital staff, but they are not necessarily so for children. Whilst it is appropriate that hospitals are patient-friendly where there is no alternative to inpatient treatment, most children prefer to be at home. Ways have to be found to devolve decision making and control into the community and away from the inflexibility of a building-based service if the long term care of disabled children is to be centred within their families. This is especially true when they require no medical treatment. However there are already signs of change.

The 1998 National Health Service Executive paper on good practice for children with learning disabilities emphasises the importance of understanding and meeting their emotional needs and the fundamental role of the family. Where families cannot cope, alternative family placements should be the first recourse of social services. These standards apply equally to children with physical disability.

Some Health Trusts now employ community paediatricians, community children's nurses or social workers with skills in counselling and networking, whose role in relation to families is understood to be as a supporter and facilitator. The kind of skills necessary are different from those required in a clinical or residential setting. Social workers or community children's nurses do not necessarily receive particular training in disability or learning disability issues, but they do have a basic grounding in the ability to work with people in their own homes, and should have a commitment to developing services there. This implies a clear emphasis on family support, the empowerment of direct carers and the availability of necessary expertise either in the community or at the end of a hotline for generic workers who may need to obtain specialised information or advice. It does not mean families being visited by all the members of the multidisciplinary team, who may well have conflicting priorities and methods of working.

It follows from *Signposts to Success* that services such as respite care could also move towards an 'at home' model as the first priority

(NHSE, 1998). This is especially crucial where young children are concerned. Disabled children under the age of 8 are still moved 'out of county' by some social services at great expense both financially to the social services and emotionally to the child and parents. The '52 week' placements could be phased out if education and social services jointly commit themselves to a principle of caring for all children as close to their families as possible.

Many policies around respite care have been generated by small numbers of children who have serious medical needs, and who are often maintained by the use of technology or complex drug regimes. Although parents are expected to accept the risks of complex care within the home environment, other carers are frequently prevented by lack of insurance cover from doing so. This can provide health and social care providers with a rationale for failing to develop support such as family aides to the child's home, or family based respite. Modern technology will increasingly resolve some healthcare needs, but its provision should not be used as an excuse for failing to seek ways to meet the child's broader social and emotional needs. Nor should we confuse an ability to manage a mechanical device or administer a drug regime with an understanding of the medical condition or the healthcare needs of the child.

It is strange then, that someone's ability to perform a technical procedure can make the difference between the perceived appropriateness of placements. This is not to deny that there are risks involved, but to suggest that technological considerations could be dealt with after a decision about the best means of supporting a child or family have been reached on emotional, developmental, educational, social and medical grounds. If not, medical technology can develop into a barrier to integration and normality, rather than acting as it should, as an aid towards living a normal childhood.

Some highly technological solutions can only be provided on an institutional basis, in which cases there are some difficult decisions to be made about the level of risk which is acceptable, compared with the damage to quality of life which reliance on such technology can bring. Even for those with serious medical problems, it may not be sensible to try to legislate away all risk. The flight to failsafe systems owes a great deal to a developing litigious culture in which many healthcare staff operate in fear of being sued for negligence. As such they are perhaps less willing to engage in open discussions with patients or their relatives about uncertainties and possibilities. Decisions which weigh safety against quality or length of life should not be left entirely to medical staff. Those who love and care for a severely disabled child need informed discussion about the risks involved in caring for them at home, in order to reach difficult decisions which weigh risk of death or further disablement against quality of life. Some children may be able to reach such decisions themselves.

That some severely disabled children may die at an earlier age as a result of not spending their lives in hospital wards may be a more acceptable outcome than removing all children at such risk into institutional environments. Making policies based on 'worst case scenarios' may not represent the best solution for all children. It might represent a better and more equitable use of healthcare resources to provide more personal support for people at home in the form of trained healthcare professionals. In her work on rationing in the National Health Service, Goldring talks of the 'embarrassment of high tech' for the few while a great many others are denied help (Goldring, 1998).

Towards inclusive education

Arguments in support of inclusive education have been published widely throughout the world for many years, so there is no shortage of practical advice available (Dunn, 1968; Valletutti, 1969; Hegarty, 1982, 1987; Wang *et al.*, 1992; Jonsson, 1994; Stainback & Stainback, 1994; Casey, 1994; Vargo & Vargo, 1995; Brown *et al.*, 1989; Villa & Thousand, 1995; Muthukrishna, 1996). The main arguments which are still put forward as reasons not to include were reviewed in Chapter two, although they were presented in the knowledge that this overtly intellectual and rational debate is undermined by much less reasonable underlying dynamics which maintain segregation. There are perceived advantages for the majority in maintaining an unequal society, which are rarely openly acknowledged or discussed. Even though we know that these less reasonable dynamics are powerful, it is necessary to have clear principles and a vision of what kind of educational system would work. We also need to find ways of countering the power issues which maintain inequalities.

Hegarty argues from reviewing the literature that children can cope very well if the school environment is positive. He argues that integration means school reform, not pupil placement. In other words education should be about fitting schools to pupils not socialising pupils to pre set norms and behaviour (Hegarty, 1987). Lewis recommends that *all* children could be welcomed and valued so that there is little or no need for specific programmes to encourage tolerance, which can patronise the disabled children who are the subjects of them (Lewis, 1995). This means working on ways to respect all the children, including recognising and respecting their differences.

Removing children with severe difficulties from education in their local school deprives both them and their communities from knowing and learning from each other. On both groups entering adulthood, segregation results in calls for ' normalisation', 'integration' or 'disability awareness training', all of which emphasise that disabled people are somehow odd, have to adjust to fit in and require special understanding. Parents of children away from home can also become isolated from local communities. There is no doubt some children require extra support in the form of ancillary staff, special equipment and support from paramedical and medical staff, but there is no reason why these things cannot be provided within regular schools.

Physical reforms to schools are at once the easiest to work out, and the most intractable to achieve if the will is lacking. They involve accessible environments, not simply to enter the front door but to move round the whole building, adequate heating and lighting, fire escapes, as well as specialised equipment such as loop systems. Accessible toilets could be available throughout the building and not in a single location apart from others. Such structures enable disabled children to participate on a more equal basis and keep reliance on the goodwill of other pupils to a minimum. Achieving social acceptance is easier if disabled pupils are not seen as detracting from the needs of their non-disabled contemporaries. For the same reason of social acceptance, teachers need to learn to be even handed. Too benign an approach to a disabled child, out of misplaced sympathy, can alienate them from their fellow pupils as well as falling into the trap of lowering the expectations placed on them. The students who were interviewed were particularly critical of teachers who did not expect that they could achieve normal levels of attainment.

Traditional teaching methods may need review. Single teachers seeking to meet the needs of groups of 30 or more diverse children in a classroom are increasingly inappropriate given the opportunities presented by computer technology and distance learning. The teacher as part of a team which includes other teachers, classroom assistants, technicians and parents, rather than the teacher as soloist, is a much more helpful model for the future, but requires different organisation and structures in schools. Team teaching is likely to result in higher quality education than solo teaching, in that it requires much more attention to planning lessons and organising material, and is subject to day-to-day peer review.

Some groups of children may benefit from being educated together for parts of the curriculum. Braille users, for example, may benefit from time together just as musically gifted children may have separate lessons during part of the day. The effects of such segregation, even for sound educational reasons, cannot be underestimated in social terms. Both of the above groups may suffer teasing because of their special treatment and children need to learn the reasons for it early in life. There are developmental considerations here, of course: visible disabilities are easier for children to understand than hidden or learning disabilities; but Lewis's research indicates that children are more tolerant of disability when they have a better understanding of what it means (Lewis, 1995).

The advances of modern technology such as video, multi-media and computer technology enable learning to become an individualised process in terms of speed, customisation and interactiveness. This is exciting for all learners, but it offers particular opportunities for disabled pupils to access learning on the same basis as their non-disabled peers. Active, individual learning packages can be introduced for all children.

Such individual portfolios built up for each pupil, disabled or non-disabled, enable teachers to identify gaps and encourage learning in necessary directions. There is no need for all the children in the class to learn at the same pace, nor for a child who is good at one subject to be held back because they are less competent in another field. Computers enable difficult lessons to be rerun as necessary, and do away with much of the ridicule that accompanies traditional teaching where failure to understand can be very public. This does not mean the curriculum has to be different, but that by the use of different teaching methods and materials the *same curriculum* can be accessed by different means.

This is an important distinction, since the complaint of many of the disabled young people was that they were excluded from learning because of the lower expectations placed on them through their inability to learn by traditional methods. Building up portfolios of achievement reinforces success and enables children to demonstrate the things they are good at. As the respondents in Chapter one so graphically demonstrated, there is considerable value in identifying the things that can be achieved.

The *Guardian* reported the response of teachers and pupils in a school in Bristol to the introduction of computers:

> 'They enable the children to be highly motivated, and they save an awful lot of time. Rather than spending four hours drafting and rewriting a story, good computer usage frees the children to do more challenging work. Computers take the drudgery out of learning, and children can see their results very quickly.'

> (*Guardian*, 10th February 1998)

Pupils were equally enthusiastic and teaching staff claimed the advantages are not simply academic, but that computers also improve attendance as children enjoy their learning. This begs questions about whether teachers are able to replicate the enjoyable aspects of computer based learning and integrate them into their own practice!

These changes, which are of benefit to all learners, are held back more by the failure of adult teachers to get to grips with new technology, as well as a lack of imagination among school managers, than by any lack of enthusiasm among the younger generation. Computer technology can also be used to communicate between schools, and between schools and specialist centres providing opportunities for distance learning for both staff and pupils. Specialist teaching, where necessary, can be accessed over distance and pupils do not need to move themselves to benefit from it. Specialist teachers can stay in touch with each other both for support and to disseminate good practice and new ideas. Even within the same school e-mail can be used as a means of communication between teacher and pupils, individually and on a group basis, and among pupils themselves; it may be particularly useful as a bridge between deaf and hearing children, for those without speech or for those who think at different speeds.

There are, of course, concerns that learning by computer prevents children from learning to interact with each other socially. This is unproven. Children play computer games together as well as on a solo basis, and computer enthusiasts talk to each other. Yet lack of understanding of computer technology may increasingly deprive children of the tools for dialogue and interaction. Nor does better use of technology preclude making use of traditional teaching as and when appropriate. The use of different methods can be explained and justified either in educational or social terms in each case. Traditional classroom teaching probably did little to enhance social or co-operative behaviour. It is in the playground, the street and the home that social and antisocial behaviours are learned, and it is there that far too much has been left to chance.

Deaf children face particular barriers since their first language may be different from hearing children, or even from their own parents. Recognition of sign language as a resource for both hearing and deaf children, and its introduction into school curricula as a second language for hearing children, would go a long way toward breaking down this particular barrier.

It was noted in Chapter two that there were instances where disabled children did well in examinations in segregated schools, but suggested this might be at some social cost. Such instances needed to be dissected and analysed so that the ingredients for success could be replicated in mainstream schools. For example, pupils at the RNIB New College were noted by OFSTED in 1997 to have achieved GCSE results at twice the national average. Last year all its sixth formers went on to university (*Guardian* 4th February 1998). Clearly, the school is successfully enabling the children to achieve, and to go on to higher education.

The ingredients for success were described by OFSTED as follows. All course work was available in Braille. This included raised maps for those studying geography, and raised diagrams in maths and science. Information technology was considered vital, with talking computers, and computers to translate into Braille. Class sizes were small. There is, of course, much debate in education about class size, but most people accept the common sense view that teaching in smaller groups is better than being taught in large numbers for most subjects. In the evenings pupils learned skills such as cooking, financial management and using public transport. It is significant, bearing in mind the comments made by the Preston students, that these skill sessions were not allowed to interrupt the normal school curriculum. Replicating these ingredients in local schools would mean that visually disabled children could have the benefits of sound educational support without having to attend boarding school and be isolated from their family and community to obtain it.

If such support were available in the local mainstream schools, any decision to leave home for schooling would be based on a real choice. Mainstream schools will undoubtedly maintain that they do not have the resources to match this kind of specialist input, and on an individual level they may be right. Nonetheless many education authorities are making resource choices based on the relatively easy option of sending disabled children away from home and simply footing the bill, instead of making plans to utilise funding to enable the same quality of education to be provided locally.

Finally, schools need to tackle the issue of bullying. It is false to assume that special schools provide safety from this. There are two levels on which this needs attention: one is bullying in general, which is a problem for most children at some time in their schooling, and the second is that bullying which relates to disability. It is important that disabled children are encouraged to understand that while their disabling condition may be the vehicle for their being bullied, it is not essentially the reason for it. They might be bullied anyway. This is a difficult distinction. It is also difficult to work out strategies to tackle bullying related to disability which do not make things worse. Suggestions that the bullying pupils are given disability awareness lessons, for example, so that they gain a better understanding of the disabling condition, can easily backfire and result in disabled children becoming even more vulnerable or regarded as objects of pity rather than equals.

Bullying, however, reflects the ethos of a school and of the wider community. Disabled children are more likely to avoid it if they are a contributing and valued part of the group. They may also have to learn not to mind name calling, which means feeling positive about themselves. Teasing only hurts when it is directed at some feature or behaviour which the individual themself feels unhappy or uneasy about. As described earlier, vigorous attempts to change their appearance cosmetically teaches disabled children that there is something about their bodies which is not acceptable. This renders them particularly susceptible to teasing about it.

Children in residential schools are especially vulnerable. Being away from home and community means they cannot benefit from the support of family and friends. This makes bullying easier, and it also makes it easier for those staff who engage in abusive behaviour. This is more than just a physical separation from support. Disabled children are not in residential school because they are seen to deserve better, but because their local community and school cannot (or will not) cope with their needs. By implication, those children who are away from home are seen to be valued and cared about less, and are therefore easier targets for would-be abusers.

The widespread problem of bullying in schools is not an issue which concerns only children. It reflects a blame culture which permeates many schools. This was highlighted in 1998 by the case of Anthony Ratcliffe, a teacher who successfully sued his employers when driven out of his job by bullying. Research at Surrey University claimed that a fifth of teachers had experienced bullying at work, commonly by headteachers or deputies (Thomas, 1998). Since bullying is only a part of the spectrum of violence, it is not simply a matter for schools but one of wider political concern. In relation to domestic violence, Mullender (1996) identifies three levels of prevention: broad public education, encouraging victims to seek help and ensuring that their needs are met when they do.

'By teaching young people or the general public that male abuse is unacceptable and will not be tolerated there may be a primary prevention role in preventing some abuse from ever happening. Social workers and probation officers who spread Zero Tolerance attitudes in all their contact with service users and the general public ... can play a role here.'

(p 259)

She adds that it might help if such workers felt supported by a climate of official backing and generally heightened awareness.

Conclusion

Inclusion requires organisations to change in many ways: in making their value basis explicit, for example, and in taking practical measures to extend a welcome to all children; yet it is even more complicated than that. Organisations cannot operate in isolation from each other. To integrate a disabled child into a local school, for example, requires commitment not just from the school, but from the local library, the planning department, the general practitioner and community nursing service and social services. Disabled children are more likely than most groups to fall into the gaps between the growing number of agencies responsible for commissioning and delivering education, health and welfare services. The mechanisms for managing joint working already exist in the form of Joint Care Planning Teams and Area Child Protection Committees, which have well established mechanisms for co-ordinating practice across agencies, and need only to extend such practices to recognise and include disabled children.

Welfare, health and educational services in the UK are currently undergoing substantial changes that show no signs of slowing down. This can be seen as the opportunity for people to exert influence both on policy and practice. The challenge is for all the complex range of commissioning and service providers to work from the same principles.

Chapter 6

Disabled Children: Excluded Citizens?

'Surely the representation and exploration of human experience is incomplete as long as disability is either missing or misrepresented.'

(Jenny Morris, 1991, p 85)

'It would take me a long time to understand how systems inflict pain and hardship in people's lives and to learn that being kind in an unjust system is not enough.'

(Helen Prejean, *Dead Man Walking*, 1993, p 8)

'Boys and Girls come out to play
The moon does shine as bright as day
Leave your supper and leave your sleep
Join your playfellows in the street.'

(Nursery rhyme)

Introduction

If disabled children are to achieve citizenship they require changes to their social lives, to the sort of medical help they receive and to their educational opportunities; but they also have to lay claim to the right to influence their own destinies. In the light of the student experiences discussed in Chapter one, this means working toward things which may be taken for granted for non-disabled children, such as equality of access and opportunity, and a non-discriminatory environment. These are aspects of social justice.

Attitudes towards inclusion are shaped by society. This final chapter explores citizenship as it relates to disabled children, before describing the kind of changes which might improve their situation. If they are to cease to be the 'objects of concern' highlighted in the Cleveland Report (Secretary of State for Social Services, 1988, p 25), this means more than improving the quality of existing services. Participation as citizens means becoming part of the decision making processes which determine the sort of society we live in, and hence what kind of services are desirable. This fundamental shift involves a change of identity as well as breaking into the vicious cycle of discrimination.

Two important messages have to be transmitted and understood, and the connections between them made and analysed. First, children have rights as children and not just as proto-adults; and second, disabled people's lives are very much worth living.

This means giving disabled children a voice. As we have seen, this voice can be retrospective, if adults are able to recognise that aspects of their own upbringing were damaging or could have been better managed. The disabled students represented a group able to point out possibilities for change, and to do so on a comparable basis with non-disabled contemporaries. Disabled children and young people, their parents and advocates now need to find ways to become better integrated into policy making bodies, from school management committees to the House of Commons, so that this wealth of ideas is not squandered.

Disabled children and citizenship

In trying to develop a model of childhood, theorists have postulated two main sets of ideas, which can be described as 'protectionist' (in which children are seen as innocents in need of adult guidance) and 'liberationist' (in which children are seen as oppressed by adult control). The former model suggests adults have a duty of care and control, while the latter sees children as able to be self-determining. In practical terms the protectionist model is illustrated by adults making children go to school and setting the curriculum, while the liberationist model would leave them free to decide for themselves. Protectionists support laws setting the age of criminal responsibility, the age of consent for sexual intercourse, employment regulations and so on, while liberationists regard these as needless impositions which deny children the same rights as adults. These opposing perspectives underpin a great deal of childcare literature and thinking, and are usefully discussed by Harding in a companion volume in this series (Harding, 1998).

There is no evidence that protagonists of either model have taken into account a perspective on disability issues. Within the extreme perspectives outlined above, one can put forward a view of the child as neither innocent, nor oppressed but as a developing human being learning to function within an established social structure. This model recognises the inter-dependency of individuals and their environment and the capacities of both to change. Any individual has potential, and while no-one's path is determined entirely by birth, life-chances are influenced by a range of environmental factors. So long as childhood is regarded as a transitional state en route to becoming an adult, investment in children may be related to the perceived value of the adults it is thought they may become. Being born with, or developing a disabling condition, works negatively in a society which discriminates against disabled people. This is not a particularly pleasant way of thinking about the issue, as it reduces human beings to the status of commodities, with more or less value in society. Nevertheless, understanding these dynamics ties the interests of disabled adults and children closely together.

The pressures of modern society mean most children and adults find themselves looking to plan and secure their futures, in terms of schooling, examinations, careers, mortgages, pensions, or long-term residential care; all of which can be at the expense of current enjoyment. These pressures are particularly heavy for parents of disabled children, whose futures can seem so uncertain. Nevertheless it is worth reminding ourselves that children live in the present, as well as being en route to adulthood, and that the pleasure of childhood itself should not be lost.

As well as a relationship with the immediate environment, the individual has a more formal relationship with the State. Citizenship is not automatic; it has to be attained and its terms negotiated. The ethos of this book is that whatever view of citizenship is adopted, it should apply equally to disabled and non-disabled children. However, this notion of equality in citizenship may run counter to views which equate citizenship with contribution, and make rights conditional on acceptance of duties. The effect of the New Right and of twenty years of market-driven politics has been to emphasise the concept of rights as attaching to the consumer with money to spend or goods to exchange. Entitlement has been exchanged for obligation, so that the dependent citizen has the responsibility to keep their dependency on benefits to a minimum (Lister, 1990). The Labour Party have not altered this focus on personal investment in individual futures: citizens should expect to pay for their own higher education, and provide for their own old age. It follows that dependent citizens should not expect to share the same privileges as contributing citizens, nor enjoy so high a social status. While disabled children are construed by the majority of society as non-contributing, this model implies they will also be perceived as non-participating.

Disabled children need to develop a new relationship in which they are not excluded as having 'special needs' but seen as girls and boys with a range of hopes, wishes and dreams like any others. The social model of disability is helpful in this respect, since it leads to thinking in terms of social, environmental and attitudinal barriers to those aspirations, and ways to dismantle them, rather than focusing on the child as the problem. Removing barriers will enable more children to participate and contribute, creating a reciprocal relationship rather than a dependent one.

Modern society is a complex web of checks and balances. Laws, customs and practices regulate relationships between individuals and groups: men and women, employers and employees, road users and pedestrians. Both adults and children are constrained by rules, from laws to socially determined interactions. These 'rules' of social engagement have to be learned if individuals are to fit in. Babies are self-centred and aware only of meeting short term need; in maturity our decisions are supposed to take account of long term consequences, and their effects on our relationships with others. Such decision making demands an ability to achieve abstract thinking and is honed by experience. It follows that it should improve with age, as should accountability for one's actions. In a healthy society members exercise individual and collective responsibility.

There is not any particular age at which social learning starts or ceases, but there are of necessity arbitrary legal ages by which time individuals are held accountable for their actions. While arguments will continue about the appropriate age for any particular right or duty, or indeed about the number of such laws, such a regulatory framework is necessary.

Since these relationships, checks and balances are artificially determined and culturally specific, those who determine and operate them wield considerable power. Yet the responsible adult who has no authority cannot exercise either care or control. It is no use, for example, charging social services with the duty to protect children, unless they have some power to take action.

Children are developing human beings, whose abilities, knowledge and power grow as they get older. Within a developmental perspective it is easier to achieve a balance between the theoretical polarities of protection and liberation, and recognise that children of any age are in need of a measure of protection, care and guidance. These needs are shared by adults, who are also vulnerable to, for example, violent crime, ill health and impenetrable bureaucracies. Yet protection is only one side of the coin: if a society is to learn, be creative, change and grow, then people need to experiment, take risks, and gain experience.

Children of all ages make decisions in some matters, from the breast feeding baby to the rebellious adolescent. The responsible adult enables and teaches children to make better choices. What is crucial for the social inclusion of disabled children is that their impairment does not become a negative factor. Their rights to make decisions should reflect those of their non-disabled siblings, even if the means by which they signal their choices may be different. Adherence to a particular culture or religion may be less important for children these days, as many of them are growing up more used to interaction in a multi-cultural environment than their parents. In any case, achieving some distance from parental control is part of growing up. It is important that disabled children are not forced into greater degrees of compliance than their able-bodied contemporaries simply because their disabling condition makes them easier to control. If being disabled impedes their socialisation into responsible and informed decision makers, they are more likely to be excluded.

It is not only parents who may exercise more control over disabled children than is necessary. Professionals can sometimes take over. A disabled child is at risk of too much attention being paid to the future, at the expense of present pleasure, self-exploration or of participating with others of his age in play, education or making mischief.

The United Nations Convention, ratified by the UK in 1991, accords all children the right to freedom of expression, association, privacy and access to information. These objectives may be harder when the child is disabled. It is less easy to gain both direct experience and guidance. Adults do not always consciously prepare disabled children for the same futures that they envisage for those without impairments. The students in Chapter one reported being insufficiently encouraged, denied opportunities at school and kept in ignorance about sexual relationships. As a result development may be delayed. If adults choose for them, disabled children can be denied opportunities to practise the skills of decision making. This can result in disabled youngsters failing to develop the confidence to self determine. Communication is also more likely to be neglected. It is unfortunately the case that establishing appropriate means of communication only occurs for some children as a result of suspected abuse, at which time the stress involved compounds the difficulty. The UN Convention's rights to privacy and freedom of association are also much more likely to be curtailed for disabled children, especially those in residential care.

While adults have a role to play in socialising the next generation, it is also important to acknowledge that in a changing and developing society, they should remain alive to new values and ideas. Anything else would be brainwashing. There is, of course, a necessary balance between social stability and the pressure to modernise, so that changes in the way a democratic society operates are achieved through discussion, persuasion, consensus and legislation. These processes inevitably favour the interests of some groups over others, and disabled children have had comparatively little influence. This is a vicious circle, in which exclusion from social, educational and employment opportunities perpetuates powerlessness, if only by instilling low self-esteem. The challenge for disabled children and their advocates is to determine the best way to enter the debate and close the gap between the position of disabled and non-disabled children.

Strategies for change

This book argues that disabled children are excluded not because of soundly evidenced rational arguments but because of continuing prejudices and beliefs about disabled children and the adults they may become.

In summary these prejudices are that:

- disabled children cannot be included as full citizens since they are non-contributing, dependent members of society, who will continue to represent a drain on services;

- unlike other disadvantaged groups they are unlikely to cause a crime wave, disrupt communities or grow up to take revenge, nor do they have the vote. They can be marginalised with impunity;

- in a hierarchy based on strength, beauty, sexual attraction and the ability to fight and to reproduce, disabled children are not equals and do not deserve to be treated as such;

- if disability cannot be eliminated through selective abortion, medical science should make every effort to transform disabled children into non-disabled children, even if this is only cosmetic.

It follows that any strategies for change must deal with these prejudices as well as continuing to provide reliable research evidence of the facts. In what follows I shall break down the task in the hope that it will appear less daunting, and in the belief that everyone has a role to play in challenging oppression. Achieving social inclusion means changes to many aspects of our lives. Personal identity, family and social relationships, are considered, together with possible roles for researchers and disabled adults.

Acquiring a positive identity

For disabled children change means acquiring identities in the eyes of society which are active, and which acknowledge gender, race, class, age and sexuality. These are attributes by which most people are defined and define themselves, but which are rarely applied to disabled children, who continue to be defined within a unitary identity that is largely 'degendered, asexual, culturally unspecific and classless' (Priestley, 1998a, p 220). Age and gender are the most significant factors in determining who children are and who they identify with (Lewis, 1995). Those of us who are no longer six or seven years old tend to forget the importance of age to children, who commonly sign themselves 'Shaun, aged five and a half' and establish their own age and their companions' with more pride and less embarrassment than the average grown up. Most of this book has referred to disabled children, rather than disabled boys or girls, men and women. This is not simply because it is shorter and neater: it also reflects the way we conceptualise disabled children as without gender.

There may be additional complications for disabled black children since experiencing both racism and disablism can make it even harder to understand what is going on or how to get help. There is a great deal of confusing intellectual debate about whether oppression is multiple, parallel or hierarchical, which is not especially helpful. It is clear, however, that a disabled black girl is in a smaller minority than a disabled white girl in the UK and she may find it that much harder to find other children like herself. Disability considerations have often overridden racial and cultural needs in placing children in special schools or residential homes.

In reviewing 50 years of services for children, Stevenson notes that

'tales of black children scrubbing themselves at bath time to become white are now familiar.'

(Stevenson, 1997, p 9–10)

She implied that improvements had been made since then but it is important any such progress extends to *all* children. The student who rubbed her face with floor cleaner should remind us there is no room for complacency. Fifty years of childcare have taught us some lessons about helping black children to be proud of their identity. These should not be lost when the child in question is disabled.

In terms of gender identity, even drawing attention to the fact that disabled children consist of boys and girls helps create a more individual different mental image of them. It may also raise questions about the implications of our failure to use a gender analysis in relation to disabled children. Using neutral language 'hides' girls and women more than men and boys, since readers of both sexes are still accustomed to think first in male terms.

Accepting disabled adults and children as full citizens also means accepting that they have sexual identities and should be included in what Plummer has called 'sexual citizenship' (Plummer, 1995, p 150). This is difficult to achieve. The sexuality of disabled children is still widely denied, and seems to be viewed in terms of their vulnerability to sexual abuse, a passive victim role. Banim and Guy suggest disabled young people receive very conflicting messages at the moment: adolescence being about risk and sexual activity, while disability is about tragedy and passivity (Banim & Guy, 1995). Yet it is clear both from the experiences reported in Chapter one, and from the respondents in Shakespeare's study, that disabled young people are sexually active, even allowing for the bravado one might expect to be generated by being interviewed on the subject.

Becoming a parent is widely regarded as evidence of adulthood and normality, separating adults from children on the one hand and normal people from sexual deviants on the other. Disabled young people who have fears about their 'normality' may be tempted to have children simply to prove that they can. In this respect they are no different from many young people who associate parenthood with being grown up, and expect to be treated differently as a result. Jenny Morris admits to the satisfaction she derived from taking her daughter shopping, since it identified her as a mother and not a disabled person.

> 'I myself prefer to go shopping with my child because her presence at my side gives me, I mistakenly think, a passport into the world of normal people. To assert that I am a mother is to distance myself from the abnormality of being disabled.'
>
> (Morris, 1991, p 36)

This association of motherhood and normality may be particularly true in more traditional cultures:

> 'I'm Jordanian ... to be a woman in the Middle East is to have children, the two things go together, you are not considered a woman if you can't have kids, that's the crux of it.'
>
> (Jazz, quoted in Shakespeare *et al.*, 1996, p 61)

Whilst of course disabled people can be good parents, and they should not be denied the right because of inadequate support, it is important that this step is undertaken as an informed choice, and not as something vital to a healthy and happy adulthood.

A positive identity also means feeling good about the way we look. This is more complicated than simply liking our physical appearance; it is an elaborate cultural construction based on changing style and footwear and clothing which are appropriate to age and social group. Although letting go of the fashion ideology might be seen as liberating, children and young people like to belong and disabled children can find themselves excluded. High street shops may not be accessible. Advertisements, catalogues and shop window displays for clothes rarely feature disabled models. It may be harder for children with communication difficulties to negotiate with shop assistants, and blind children need time to have clothing described to them. As a result, parents may take more responsibility for choosing for disabled children which can result in them looking and feeling out of step with their contemporaries. The existence of a visible disabling condition which marks a child out as different makes it even more important to ensure that he or she can conform with their peer group in terms of style. This extends to nails, hair style, body piercing, jewellery, make up, perfume, bedroom design, music and magazines.

The media have a key role to play in improving the visibility of disabled boys and girls, especially in eradicating the twin stereotypes of 'plucky little crip' and 'tragic victim'. This does not mean asking writers and producers to spoon-feed us with moral tales about the horrors of special education or how it feels to be excluded. It entails the more subtle, more regular inclusion of disabled boys and girls as integral parts of all kinds of stories, simply so we get used to seeing them around.

This emphasis on acquiring identities relating to race, gender, age and appearance does not make it any less necessary for disabled children to acquire a disability identity which is positive. Shakespeare and his colleagues stress that this is not the same as coming to terms with impairment, but involves a similar acceptance and public affirmation of self to the process of 'coming out' as gay (Shakespeare *et al.*, 1996, p 50).

Nor should we lose sight of the fact that identity is more than belonging to a category. It is about developing individual distinctiveness: a journey of self awareness that starts with being able to recognise the effects of other people's behaviour, and relegate it to its proper place.

> 'It has taken me a long time to wake up to the fact that I am not the problem, they are. At college they use to pick on me because of the way I looked but I've got more than them. I have a personality. I realise that it's what's inside a person that counts.'

> (Preston respondent)

Identity is not something imposed externally, but an interaction between the individual and their environment. Priestley (1998b) reminds us that children are

> 'by no means passive in their construction of their identities. These are not the passive, vulnerable children of the Dickensian novel or the socio-medical research literature.'

> (Priestley, 1998b)

The respondents in Chapter one demonstrated strategies to influence or resist, although not all had positive outcomes. Priestley cites a number of girls and boys in his study who made use of their disability when it proved convenient. For example, one boy who hates science tells how he 'mucks about' on the way to the lesson and then plays the disabled role when he arrives late by telling the teacher that his wheelchair is slow. We are not told how other pupils responded to this!

Family relationships

Many disabled children are born to, and raised by, non-disabled adults. Many parents want their son or daughter to grow up to be like them. This can create enormous pressure on both parent and child. Children normally wish to please their parents and can grow up feeling that they have let them down simply because they are different. Non-disabled parents of disabled children cannot easily act as role models. Unlike black parents, for example, they are unable to share their own personal coping mechanisms for dealing with teasing, bullying and other forms of oppressive behaviour. There has yet to be any real debate in this country about the needs of non-disabled parents raising children with impairments. Furthermore, while no-one would seriously suggest removing disabled children from their non-disabled parents to provide that experience, there is room for exploring the advantages of this when it comes to selecting foster carers. The disability movement can help address issues for disabled children who find themselves at odds with parents, or treated differently from their siblings.

Parents from minority ethnic groups may find themselves even more cut off from advice, support and positive role models, despite the relatively high numbers of disabled children born into these communities (Kurtz, 1993). This means examining issues like racism in service provision and differing cultural understandings of disability. Whatever such cultural differences may be, the principle of equality between disabled and non-disabled children remains the same, and should serve as a starting point for discussion with parents about ways in which their disabled children may become disadvantaged.

Help for parents has tended to focus on an explanation of the medical condition, an assessment of the child's educational potential and advice about extra help for the parents, either in the home or by providing respite care elsewhere. A more positive approach would involve helping parents to understand what the issues are for a child growing up with a disabling condition in an able-bodied world, and to support them in dealing with these. This may mean constantly demanding answers from MPs, councillors and service providers which focus on the quality of service, not the shortcomings of the child.

Girls and boys have a right to enjoy their childhood and the pleasures of growing up. Disabled children can easily be denied a normal childhood by concentration on problems relating to their disability and on fears for their future. Parents who believe that their children will be able to survive without them need to accept that the children will be able to make their own choices about lifestyle when they reach adulthood, and to raise them accordingly. Hiding the child in cotton wool for as long as possible will not help in the long term. Children whose parents do not allow them to grow up or to make other friends and contacts outside the home, are likely to fare far worse when their parents are no longer there than those who make progress toward independence while their parents are there to support the enterprise. This is no different for young disabled men and women.

Developing a better understanding of the effects of impairment and the ways in which society disables should enable parents to become more confident and search out the appropriate resources and services to enhance the lives of their children, rather than making things worse. This entails challenging medical and educational experts rather than giving in to pressures to change the child. It means an early acceptance of the disability, and a diversion of energy into working out the child's best future rather than striving to put right the 'wrong' by heroic medical intervention or expensive unproven therapy. This does not mean accepting limitations – indeed the evidence of this study is that disabled children should be encouraged to follow normal leisure, social and educational pathways – but that children should make their journeys as themselves.

In terms of the child's behaviour there are two contrasting issues to appreciate. On the one hand, behaviours resulting from the impairment can easily be attributed to other factors by adults who do not have direct experience of it. For example, a visually disabled child might prefer to walk behind another person to watch their feet as a guide. Her parents need to understand she is not simply 'lagging behind'. French tells how despite living in the same house for 16 years she does not recognise her neighbours. They failed to understand that she could not see them approaching and so was unable to indulge in the kind of passing pleasantries that sighted people take for granted. As a child her sighted parents could not always understand:

> 'as a small child I had a dislike of going out on windy days. My mother, no doubt exasperated, asked me why this was so to which I replied "the wind gets in my way". I do not remember this incident but it is recalled, as an amusing family story, to show what a quaint and peculiar child I was. As a visually disabled adult I know exactly what I meant.'

(French, 1998)

The student who reported looking at the ground in order to avoid accidents in his wheelchair could easily be misconstrued as being antisocial. Many children who have difficulty eating or drinking will avoid accepting hospitality in case they make a mess, but their refusal can be seen as rude. Some will avoid social situations altogether when eating and drinking are expected to be integral parts of the occasion. Deaf children who lip read can only read one face at a time, and may appear to be staring rudely. In a crowd, they may seem distracted when they are in fact excluded. Such children can sometimes compensate by hogging the floor somehow, if they do get the opportunity.

It is distressing for children constantly to have to explain their disabilities and their effects to others, and parents have to find ways to deal with this which do not diminish the child's self esteem. Cold finger buffets are more easily managed than food requiring knife and fork dexterity, for example. Children who use sign language to communicate may prefer to keep their hands free, so the kind of parties which involve carrying food and drink about are unhelpful.

This means that parents need to understand their child's actions even if the child cannot explain. Since disabled children do not have the experience of being able-bodied, they may not learn the reasons for their different behaviours, nor even appreciate that they are different, until they are older. Links with disabled adults could help both parents and children develop better understandings of what it means to be disabled.

On the other hand, behaviours which in a non-disabled child would signal pain, unhappiness, homesickness, or alert an adult to the possibility of bullying or abuse can sometimes be wrongly attributed to an impairment. Changes in behaviour or attitude deserve investigation. If a child suddenly stops being able to sleep, refuses to eat, develops tantrums, stops wanting to go to school, gets tearful, or develops bruising or bleeding, these should alert parents to the possibility that something is wrong.

Parents of any child have a great deal to learn, and there are clearly additional lessons for those whose child is different in some way from the majority. The media could play a part in education for and about disabled people. There is much information in newspapers week by week giving advice about gardening, cookery and financial management, whereas advice on relationships is largely confined to problem columns, or 'Agony Aunt' features. This effectively means that issues about human relationships are dealt with only after things have gone wrong, suggesting that most people would normally be expected to know instinctively what to do and how to behave. If a cookery column confined its advice to rescue operations for spoiled dishes we would consider it unbalanced. There could be a case for a 'parents page', written in the same positive and forward thinking way that cooking and investments are dealt with. This could easily include features on diversity, disability and making friends.

It would be helpful if organisations of parents were to accept collective responsibility to evaluate the appropriateness and quality of services more carefully, rather than simply demanding *more*. This does not just apply to education and health, but to the whole range of facilities and organisations which a child can use: crèches, clubs, playgrounds, parks, buses, trains, planes, libraries, cinemas, theatres, shops, cafes, restaurants, discos, sports centres, radio and television. Moving to thinking about the wider issues of how society disables would enable children to be helped in more positive and different ways. Links between parents' organisations and those of disabled people could help, especially if the alliance were approached in a spirit of mutual learning, and with an acceptance that there is more than one legitimate viewpoint.

Parents' organisations have a key role to play in reversing the 'rationing game' which creates pressure to exaggerate the problems caused by children in order to secure service provision (see Chapter two). Casting the child as the family burden damages self esteem. Ending this particular vicious circle will entail a fundamental shift in the ways in which service commissioners and providers work. Parents, professionals, researchers and campaigners in the disability movement, all acting together, can generate a turnaround from services according to 'need' (as determined by the assessor) towards services which are available as of right.

If parents and other advocates make progress, disabled children will cease to be known only as tragic victims, whose only point of contact with many people is the impersonal charitable donation. There will be more disabled boys and girls in future in everyone's everyday lives. They will cease to be strangers and become individuals we know by name, not so very different from the rest of us.

Friendships

Lifestyles are changing for all children. The combined fear of traffic and child abduction mean less emphasis on playing in the street. Most disabled children can join in the new computer-based culture as well as any others. In this sense children have commonality of interest, experience and skill from which many adults may be excluded, and which over-rides physical difference. Friends at any age can be powerful allies, as well as others with whom to have fun or share grief. For a disabled child, a friend can also act as an advocate, although the term is unlikely to be used. A child will happily pose the kind of naive questions adults might not bother to ask because they anticipate a negative answer, such as: 'why can't my friend come with me?'

Children may well be best left alone to negotiate friendships, although adults can provide opportunities for interaction. Children need to learn the skills involved in making and keeping friends. In this respect there are traps into which a disabled child is more likely to fall than a non-disabled child. Their chances of lasting friendship, in childhood or later in life, are based on understanding reciprocity. It is important that disabled children are not conditioned into dependent roles, and learn to give as well as receive. Friendships can be fickle, and it helps to explain that children who change friends are not rejecting because of the disability. It also helps if children learn not to attach too much importance to name calling, and to recognise that there are usually other children to make friends with.

Sports and games are ways of making friends. Those which do not rely on physical ability could be more widely available. However, disabled girls and boys can join in physical games, and should do so on the same basis as able-bodied competitors, so that we do not have the spectacle of the boys race, the girls race and the genderless 'wheelchair' race. When I suggested this to a committee member from the local sports club, they initially replied along the lines that all wheelchairs were equal, before realising with some embarrassment that it was the occupants who were racing, and not the chairs.

The advantages of living in a technological age are increasingly equalising opportunities for all children: the capacity to learn, communicate, or be mobile is less and less dependent on physical ability. If disabled girls and boys become better educated and more socially integrated they will more readily find work. More disabled workers will decrease hostility toward disabled people as non-contributing members of society, as well as providing role models for disabled young people. The current vicious circle of segregated education, invisibility and low expectations could be broken.

There is a less optimistic side. Despite technological and scientific progress, brute force still dominates many social relationships, and children have to come to terms with it if they are to survive. It is easier to tease, bully and exclude those who seem weak and unfamiliar: those who we do not understand, and who we do not see as 'one of us'. Increasing the visibility of disabled girls and boys, letting them grow up with non-disabled children, will not stop bullying in itself, but it will at least remove fear of the unknown as the cause. Lewis's research with schoolchildren confirmed that the familiar is preferred over the unfamiliar, and was essential to fostering positive attitudes toward disabled people (Lewis, 1995). Once the majority of us accept disabled children as a natural part of society, more ordinary men and women will start to ask questions about the needless prejudice encountered by disabled people.

To run away, join in, pick on someone smaller, or to invoke a greater power are all ways to escape bullying: but these responses leave the essential hierarchical system intact, as well as damaging self esteem. These responses apply to the playground, the home and the workplace, including those workplaces in which disabled girls and boys are cared for. To make a difference to the system entails being alert to belittling behaviour when it is indulged in by others; helping to prevent children from bullying each other; setting a good example and dealing with culprits, both adults and children. It also means acting sensitively when children and young people have suffered. Skilful counselling and advice for both children and their families should always precede referrals for psychiatric help with its implications that it is they who are sick and need to change. Violence is a cultural problem and no child or adult who suffers from it should shoulder the blame.

There is a growing recognition that the approach to issues such as domestic violence and sexual abuse has to be multifaceted and should include school, so that girls and boys learn that violence is wrong. Progress can sometimes seems slow. Clearer government policies on slapping and other physical chastisements would help, but the issue remains politically contentious.

Speaking out against aggression towards pregnant women and children should have particular meaning for disabled people, as such violence can be the cause of many impairments in childhood. Condemnation of violence, included that lauded in some forms of sport, might be a useful statement from the disability movement. People raised in poverty are more likely to die or suffer disablement than children from professional backgrounds. Where such inequalities derive from political decisions they can be altered (Oppenheim & Harker 1996; Smith, 1992). Campaigning around issues such as this can unite disparate groups of people in a constructive way, since the commonality of interest serves as an integrating factor across differences which may otherwise create barriers.

The research relationship

The research agenda is changing. Researchers into disability and childhood are increasingly recognising the value of engaging with girls and boys in their studies and the next year or so will see the beginning of research publications in which disabled children have a voice. For example, there are studies in progress at the time of writing, at Edinburgh, Leeds and Nottingham Universities, which are directly engaging with disabled children, and I am also aware of independent research (Priestley, 1998a; Shakespeare & Watson, 1998; Morris, in press; Ann Craft Trust, in press). There remains much to do.

Much research concerning disability is medically orientated and quantitative, perhaps reflecting the availability of funding, and has a tendency to cast the child as the 'problem'. The relative lack of qualitative data means the voices of children, parents and professional helpers can be ignored, and distorted impressions can arise.

For example, the number of children born with impairments among the Asian population in Britain is disproportionately high, and has attracted much research interest as a result. The coincidence of disability has been variously noted with inter-marriage (consanguinity), vegetarian diets, low immunisation rates, poor ante-natal attendance and high birth incidence. Furthermore, Asian communities have been noted to make less use of health services (Balarajan & Botting, 1989; Lumb *et al.*, 1981; Kurtz, 1993; Hopkins & Bahl, 1993).

Far less account is paid to those factors which are less easily measured and more controversial, such as the attitudes of health care workers, environmental stress, the expectations and educational levels of families and the availability of appropriately-presented support and advice. There is a comparative lack of research into social support for disabled children or parents from Asian communities, but research in related areas has suggested that a number of factors may be involved, such as high levels of illiteracy (even in Asian languages), fear of aggression in inner city areas which keeps Asian women in the home, and institutional racism within white-dominated services (Patel, 1993; Kurtz, 1993). Others with whom I have discussed this issue tell me that Asian communities provide excellent services, and that the whole research agenda is predicated on distorted premises. These perceptions require some urgent research, to move us beyond the anecdotal. We need to bear in mind that racism means black disabled children may find themselves even further away from 'citizenship' than their white contemporaries.

Priestley identifies other areas which need further research, and notes optimistically that disabled children may increasingly 'find a space' in childhood research (Priestley, 1998a, p 220). He suggests that disability workers need to work on their perspectives of childhood, while childhood researchers work on their understanding of disability issues. Both need to engage more with children. Fundamentally, research should focus on children's hopes, wishes and dreams and the barriers to their achievement, rather than casting the child as the problem. This change in focus involves asking questions such as 'why is that school failing that child?' rather than the more usual 'why is that child failing at school?' It also involves replacing research into the reasons why children are unhappy to be sent away on respite schemes with research which explores more positive ways of supporting parents in raising their children without the need to send them away from home. Supporting grandparents, for example, would normally be a better choice than using strangers.

Research in the future should focus not simply on including disabled girls and boys in their own futures, but specifically on how having an impairment affects disabled children of both genders. Disabled women have achieved this distinctiveness from disabled men in a series of publications over the last two decades (Campling, 1981; Keith, 1994; Morris, 1996a). It is now important that such gender distinction is extended to children when researchers frame their projects and analyse issues. The work by Shakespeare and his colleagues is an exception in that it acknowledges and discusses gender and sexuality difference within its analysis of sexual politics. The authors acknowledge that young people are not well represented in their study; they do not extend their analysis to children, but the book represents an optimistic and pioneering start and one hopes that future funding will allow the team to address these and the raft of other issues they have raised (Shakespeare *et al.*, 1996).

Finally, bearing in mind the aim of social inclusion, researchers need not only to include the voice of disabled children in their research, but to allow them to influence the research agenda itself. This is far from straightforward, given the complexities of research funding and the various interests which research serves, and its value may need to be demonstrated in small scale studies. Moving toward this kind of co-operation in research design will take practice, especially with groups of people who have little experience of such decision-making. At the half way stage in the Preston study I held a group meeting for those students who had given individual interviews, both to get feedback and check out my thoughts so far, and to invite their suggestions on how the next phase of the research might look. They had few ideas, and found it difficult either to generalise from their own individual situations or to speculate. Clearly it is not simply a matter of inviting disabled young people to contribute: the change from 'subject' to 'researcher' takes practice and confidence, and perhaps needs to be underpinned by a different sort of education and the self belief that one has a stake in society.

The role of disabled adults

Children do not usually campaign on their own behalf for their rights, nor do they have the vote. Their interests have to be represented by others. This raises the question about who can best adopt this role. Much advocacy on behalf of disabled children has come from professionals working with them. Educationalists and lawyers have been at the forefront of campaigns for inclusive education. Parents are some of the most powerful advocates for disabled children but, like professionals, they can also be part of the oppressive structure. Despite being designed to help, services can reinforce passivity.

Disabled adults can write their own histories, but children's stories are largely told and controlled by adult interviewers, and researchers, who may not have experienced a disability as a child. Adults, disabled and non-disabled, tend to see children as incomplete adults in whom more or less investment in time and effort is justified. Society's implicit message is that disabled children are less important than non-disabled children.

Disabled adults are central to challenging this view of disabled people as passive and non-contributing, so that disabled children have more to fall back on than pathos in their own relationship with the State. This means the active involvement of disabled adults, both in high profile campaigns and also in deepening and extending our understanding of disability issues as they involve children. There is ample evidence that disabled children are disadvantaged but there is not yet sufficient recognition or understanding of the ways in which disabled adults can be effective agents of change for children.

The challenge for the disability movement in identifying and raising issues which affect disabled children is reminiscent of that which the gay movement faces in representing the interests of young homosexuals, but it is arguably even tougher. Speaking for disabled children means representing the interests of children, some of whom are too young to speak for themselves. This may be even more daunting if it crosses ethnic or cultural differences, but it is important that minority communities are not neglected. Campaigning for others can mean intruding on someone else's perceived privacy and area of control, and it is understandable if people use this as an excuse not to interfere. It is perhaps not surprising that the campaigns to improve the lives of disabled children have centred on the public arenas of education and of abuse in residential settings, where everyone can claim a legitimate interest, rather than facing the difficulties of home life or foster care.

Unlike gender and race, which are (normally) acquired before birth and fixed for life, disability may be acquired either during childhood or as an adult, which means many campaigners for disability rights have no direct experience of childhood disability. However, disabled adults understand far better than non-disabled adults what negotiating life as a disabled person means. As such they have a legitimate right, indeed a responsibility, to participate in discussions about the lives of disabled children. Many of the difficult questions facing disabled boys and girls could be shared with those who have experience of being disabled: for example

- How can I resolve wanting to belong and fit in with my peer group with having a disabling condition that marks me out as different?

- How can I reconcile wanting to walk like other children with an acceptance that using a wheelchair is all right?

- How do I get my parents to let me go out to play with my brothers and sisters?

- How can I get the boys to see me as a girl and ask me out?

- How do I make those close to me understand how I feel and why I behave as I do?

- How do I get taken seriously?

- How do I stop people laughing at my limp/stutter/stump?

- How can I tell people I don't want to be patted on the head?

- How can I get people to help me when I need it, and not when I don't?

- How can an exclusive disability movement help me belong to my mixed community?

Just as a great deal of literature on children excludes those children who are impaired, a great deal of writing about disability rights or politics is adult focused, or includes children only as passive victims of abuse or of education. Disabled adults are now writing about themselves and their experiences and challenging non-disabled society to take their concerns on board. There is every reason for them to do this, but paying more attention to the link with the treatment of disabled children could speed progress. Many disabled men and women have written narratives which recollect their disabling experiences as children, many self-published and in the 'struggling-against-all-odds' genre, but there is little intellectual analysis which could set these within the context of the civil rights campaigns in which disabled adults are engaged. It is almost as if the issues for children are considered to be self-evident, or to follow automatically from the concerns of adults, but this is a dangerous assumption.

The disability movement is not a monolithic organisation but a dynamic interactive process, on the one hand praised for giving disabled people dignity and pride, and on the other, criticised for being sexist, racist, and dominated by wheelchair users (Campbell & Oliver, 1996). Many prominent figures, such as Christopher Reeve, have been disabled by accidents in later life, and reflect the movement's concern with the interests of adults who have been deprived of their accustomed lifestyle. To the extent that it has been dominated by the interests of articulate white men, the movement can be seen as reflecting the same hierarchies of oppression which dominate mainstream society, and it is salutary to remind ourselves that despite their own experience of oppression disabled people as a whole may be no less sexist, racist or homophobic than society at large. Such challenges should sting, and serve to fuel change.

Given that it is an adult movement it is not surprising that the disability movement has concerned itself primarily with adult issues, but it means there has been a missing dimension in the literature and in political action. This is evidenced by Campbell and Oliver's text *Disability Politics*, a history by disabled people of the last 15 years of the disability movement which contains no entry for 'children' in the index (Campbell & Oliver, 1996). This failure to connect may explain the lack of awareness of the disability movement by the students in Chapter one, although their perception that people and hostile environments were the problem should have made them natural recruits.

This is changing. There is a growing awareness of children's issues, especially among disabled researchers, who rightly take previous researchers and service providers to task for constructing a discourse around disabled children which makes them vulnerable and passive (Priestley 1998a). 'Problematic' might reasonably have been added to this list, since much published research in the area focuses less on children's needs than on identifying the burdens presented by disabled children to their parents, and finding services which work for families (Beresford *et al.*, 1996).

Including children means the disability movement's campaigns will become less straightforward. Nonetheless there are nettles to be grasped, not simply by disabled people, but by everyone with an interest in achieving change. 'Choices and Rights' by Alan Holdsworth (alias Johnny Crescendo) is widely regarded as the anthem of the disability movement, and is a fine slogan, but neither concept is simple as far as children are concerned. Some examples of these difficulties and dilemmas are:

- The right of women to choose whether or not to bear children can conflict with the argument that unborn children ought not to be aborted on the grounds of physical or intellectual impairment.

- Adults should decide for themselves whether or not to undergo cosmetic or high-risk surgery. These decisions are made on behalf of disabled children, as often as not by non-disabled adults, but how should the responsibility be allocated?

- Decisions about medical treatment and schooling have to achieve a balance between present and future advantage and disadvantage, as with all children. Neither medicine nor education are exact sciences, nor is the future accurately predictable. So who decides? Doctors, teachers, parents? Or can children make their own decisions?

- Disabled adults have the right to choose where they live, who with and who cares for them. By and large, children do not. The best they can hope for is to be allowed to express an opinion to the courts.

- Different classes or cultures may have different ideologies and ideas about disability, which may be more or less repressive. You can talk to adults, but children are their parents' responsibility. Do you apply your standards of childcare and disability rights, or theirs?

Even if these dilemmas can be resolved, there remain problems about *how* people can campaign for their rights. Effective methods have to be found which do not intimidate those they seek to influence nor alienate potential allies. Strategies for adults include political activism, belonging to disability arts groups or working in Centres for Independent/Integrated Living, but there has been little exploration of how the positive benefits of these movements can work for children. Involvement in arts projects could benefit children as well as being fun. Most children will find a niche somewhere in the worlds of drama, music, painting, sculpture or writing if they receive encouragement and if the ethos is one of enjoyment and self-expression rather than of achieving against some external standard. This will bolster self-esteem as well as providing vehicles for communication with non-disabled children. Integration by discovering and sharing common interests is far preferable to 'normalisation' methods which seek to alter appearance or physical characteristics as the route to acceptance.

Yet it sometimes seems necessary to be rude or outrageous simply to get attention. The continued failure of reason is creating the same kind of anger among disabled people as among other excluded groups, and has resulted in public demonstrations which raise the profile of their struggles. This can be a two-edged sword. Stopping the traffic gets people noticed, but it also generates hostility among those affected by the disruption. What is construed for adults as direct action, such as strikes and demonstrations, can easily be dismissed as bad behaviour if indulged in by children. A disabled adult who sits in the road is a political activist. A child who behaves the same way has 'challenging behaviour'. Yet children who organise and express their views collectively are harder to ignore than the unhappy individual. Ironically, in order not to be dismissed as childish, they may have to do so in ways which demonstrate greater levels of maturity than is usual in adult demonstrations.

Conclusion

It is now 50 years since contemporary social services for children were established, and the definition of a disabled child has not altered since the 1948 National Assistance Act. It is time to take stock and work out new directions. The changes to services suggested in this book represent a fundamental challenge to the way society as a whole operates. Simply to address service provision in isolation from developing an understanding of the wider context is unhelpful. People at the bottom of the power hierarchy may assist in the maintenance of oppressive hierarchies if they themselves are not valued. Ways to enhance their self worth within organisational structures are therefore essential ingredients to underpin organisational change.

Professional and managerial staff need to accept and understand their own power and responsibilities toward disabled children, even where these cause personal dilemmas and organisational conflicts. There is ample evidence that individuals can make a difference. Technology can also help. Computer-assisted education, communication and employment enable many more people to participate in society, and to contribute economically and intellectually. All these changes will help, but in themselves they will not be enough to address the fundamental ambivalence of society towards the inclusion of disabled people.

There is no rational basis for exclusion. Disabled children share the same right to be included as a child without impairment, and any segregated treatment should be justified with their short and long term wellbeing in mind. The literature is replete with intellectual evidence-based arguments which support inclusive services. Yet winning the argument intellectually is not enough. Nor is providing a legal framework for action, so long as it is not fully implemented, and few penalties accrue to those who fail to take the law seriously. Disabled girls and boys would not be the only beneficiaries of positive change, so we have to develop a better understanding of why society continues to resist inclusion and what needs to be done to counter this resistance. Meeting this challenge means moving beyond exhortations to 'celebrate difference' to become actively involved in decision-making at both policy and practice level. This may seem a circular argument, but it is only by breaking into the power structures that change can be effective.

This book has contributed some thoughts about the ways in which individuals and organisations may work towards a more just approach for disabled children, not as 'special' but as fellow citizens. Whether it angers or inspires, I hope it will stimulate ideas and actions. It is difficult for anyone to see the full picture, but if changes are made in the light of a common value base, they will help move us on towards a situation in which no child is socially disadvantaged because of physical differences. Inclusion means being part of the process which makes the rules. Disabled children are a long way from being in that position, but I have tried at least to give them a voice. It is for that reason that I have left the last word to them.

At the end of the interviews they were each asked 'If you had a magic wand, what would you alter, about your life, yourself, your surroundings? You can choose anything you like!' I have made no attempt to analyse these answers, some of which may strike as being very modest, but present them here both as a farewell and a thank-you for their time and as a testimony to their individuality. I hope their wishes come true!

If you had a magic wand

'I would want other people to experience, not the bullying, but the everyday problems disabled people have to come across, things like having to communicate without speaking or not being able to see or having to get about in a wheelchair.'

'A lot of things, the main thing would be that I would be able to talk properly and also I would change my looks.'

'Probably people's attitudes more than anything. Just to, I mean, not be so bloody ignorant.'

'The day when everybody's equal is probably never going to come but it would be nice.'

'That's a daft question. There's an obvious answer. I'd like to have full vision. Yes.'

'After a great deal of thought I am now not ashamed to say that if I could have a wish, it would be to have normal sight. In many ways life with poor eyesight is a struggle and I do miss out on things.'

'I would like to have the money to be able to learn to drive, to have my own car.'

'Between the ages of 13 and 16 I used to think, why me, why am I deaf and I used to dream that I was hearing. I used to think about it a lot. But when I left school I started to accept my deafness. It doesn't bother me now, so I don't dream I'm hearing now. I would like more positive deaf role models. My parents asked me about cochlea implants and I said I wouldn't like one as I'm happy the way I am.'

'We have not been allowed to go parachuting here with the student club because we are deaf, they say it's because we cannot use the radio. I would like to try it though.'

'Each sort of school having to meet some sort of standard. I know that schools have OFSTED inspections but there should be another kind of inspection just focusing on what that school provides for disabled people and how they can improve it.'

'I would like more privacy.'

'It's tempting to say right I would wake up and not be disabled any more, but honestly I don't feel I would do that, but I would like to be able to do more for myself. I would like to be able to have a personal assistant instead of my mum.'

'If I had a magic wand I would go back through my life and do it all differently.'

'I dream I can drive. I've also dreamt that I was an Olympic skier although I woke up when I came to the edge of a cliff.'

'I'd like to be a brain surgeon. How many women brain surgeons do you know?'

And finally: a day's work from Jason Awbery-Taylor

'Pete, my brother-in-law, swears that he heard a thought-processor was being built in Germany. However, I'm not convinced of its validity, so I'm trying to add about 50 or 60 words per day to the Autobiography, usually in the morning when my fingers aren't as troublesome, so I'm glad I was born with my Granddad's perseverance rather than my Dad's impatience!'

Appendix 1
Research Studies Cited in the Text

Preston research project

This book uses data from the Preston research project to illustrate and demonstrate how disabled children experience their childhoods. I embarked on this research with the aim of finding out what disabled young people themselves believed were the differences between their childhood experiences and those of their non-disabled contemporaries. They were asked to identify critical factors which either enabled their success, or created barriers to their ambitions. In particular, I wanted to explore their views about adults, including those paid to care, and to note which attitudes and behaviours were thought to be helpful or otherwise.

In seeking respondents I elected to interview ordinary young people, whose difference was a physical impairment, and in choosing to do so I was motivated by two writers in particular. The first was Jenny Morris, whose aim in *Encounters with Strangers* was to represent the lives of disabled women in a way which focused 'not just on our exclusion, but also on our survival'. In representing disabled women, including herself, she hoped to 'find a way of making our experiences visible, sharing them with each other and with non-disabled people, in a way that – while drawing attention to the difficulties in our lives – does not undermine our wish to assert our self-worth' (Morris 1996b, p 2).

I did not want to produce yet another study of disabled childhood which presented disabled children as hapless victims, so I chose subjects who were achieving normal goals as young people and sought to identify the success factors in their lives. This did not prove as simple as it appeared. Despite being university students, and therefore, by almost anyone's definition, in a successful minority group, these young people were by and large unable to acknowledge this positive perception of their situation. This hampered the search for their views about what factors facilitated their success, and it was salutary to note how persistent low self-esteem can be, once it is implanted in an individual's make up.

Not wishing to reinforce a passive disabled identity presented a problem in constructing the research questions. While a key goal was to illuminate the experience of services from the perspective of service users, the role of service user was only a part of who the children were, and one in which they may have been at their most passive. In this the students were variously patients, pupils or clients, and were necessarily experiencing each of these services as disabled children. This carried some danger that identities other than 'disabled' might be lost, and the picture painted is one of individuals who are not active participants in shaping their own lives. Countering this meant asking quite deliberate questions to extract the respondent's opinions as well as recording a narrative of events.

The second major influence in the design of the research was Nigel Parton, who, in his work on childcare services, makes the very forcible point that we persist, as a society, in legislating and making policy for the protection of children from abuse by reacting to 'worst case scenarios', those minority of cases which went horribly wrong. This is despite the fact that research into the overwhelming majority of child protection cases indicates different approaches (Parton, 1997). There have been similar dynamics operating in constructing the case for protecting disabled children from abuse, and the work of writers such as Kennedy, and Westcott and Cross contains a great deal of distressing material (Kennedy, 1989; Westcott and Cross, 1995). While it is understandable that campaigners would hope to shock service providers into making changes, telling horrific stories can make it easier, for those so inclined, to dismiss them as abnormal: something that 'could never happen here' (Churchill *et al.*, 1993).

Dismissing evidence as exceptional leaves the vast majority of professionals and organisations with the option of not examining their own practice. This book explores the reasons why service providers, normally construed as caring professionals, might wish or allow themselves to behave like this. It might be that the ability to conceptualise 'disabled children' as different from 'children' in general may underlie the apparent difference in levels of concern about their safety and wellbeing.

Method

The project lasted from October 1996 until December 1997 and was based in the University of Central Lancashire, Preston, UK. Respondents were invited through a newsletter sent by the University's specialist careers officer to all students who had registered with the careers service as disabled. This gave access to disabled students without breaking confidentiality, and left the students free to contact the researchers if they wished to participate. The letter outlined the criteria for inclusion, which included being disabled from birth or during a substantial period of their childhood. We excluded students with specific learning difficulties such as dyslexia from the study, although they formed the bulk of individuals to whom the newsletter is sent. We received 78 volunteers from the process, of whom 30 were women and 48 men.

This was far more than anticipated, and far more than we had the resources to interview. We selected 14 students, 7 men and 7 women who were at the younger end of the student age range, and so nearer to their childhoods. This was not to devalue the experience or memory of older students, but a recognition that the experiences of younger students would be less dated in terms of the services being described. Two of the respondents were Asian, the rest white. The other volunteers were invited to correspond or communicate with the research team if they wished, and were sent copies of the initial interview schedule. I received 25 letters as a result. One further respondent was Jason Awbery-Taylor, BA (Dist) Applied Social Studies. Jason had Friedrich's Ataxia, a wasting disease that steadily crippled him throughout his school and university career and finally killed him. He left behind a manuscript, 'My Life in their Hands' (Awbery-Taylor, 1994) which his parents donated to me in the hope that some of his experiences would help enlighten or encourage others. It was written using a lightwriter, at the pace of about 50 words a day.

The nature of the research means that the type of disabling condition is not relevant, except to note that the range of physical impairments included communication difficulties due to cerebral palsy and deafness. We met with the students who volunteered prior to conducting the interviews, to explain the research and our expectations, and to clarify the method of communication, recording and checking back. The majority of interviews lasted one to two hours and were audiotaped and transcribed, except where the students were deaf, when we used video recordings with voice over. Deaf respondents were offered an interpreter as the research assistant's signing was not fluent. Two opted to communicate directly and a third, who was a pure British Sign Language user, chose to use the interpreter in the first instance. Both he and the research assistant subsequently discovered they could communicate directly, a fact which helped their self-confidence.

The most difficult interview entailed a student with poor motor control, including her tongue and mouth, which made her speech hard to discern. Although she had a lightwriter she was unwilling to use it, so we considered keying in questions and answers onto a computer. This proved futile as she lacked confidence with the computer. Finally, we hit on the system of asking questions and keying in the responses ourselves, with the participant checking the accuracy of the input on the screen. Pen and paper were used to cross check. This was tiring both for the student and the interviewer, so this interview was conducted on three different days, with each session lasting about an hour and a half.

All respondents were given the opportunity to check over the audio or video tapes before they were transcribed, in case there was any material they did not wish used, or wished to amend.

The researcher used an interview schedule covering a range of areas, with no prescription either as to order or priority. Students were encouraged to offer opinion as well as narrative. The schedule was adjusted slightly during the research to encourage more of the students' views, as there was a marked reluctance to generalise beyond their own experience, or to venture conclusions from it.

To encourage discussion we also invited participants to a group discussion which took place in the middle of the research. This involved feeding back our thoughts so far, inviting comment, and soliciting from the students ideas about how we might most profitably use the second six months of our time. This discussion was recorded on audiotape and transcribed. The material generated was treated in the same way as the individual recordings.

Transcriptions, letters and Jason's autobiography were thematically analysed. Indexing categories were selected where three or more respondents made the same, or similar, points. These were then summarised into a paper, first to engender discussion with respondents during the research and later for writing up. In addition, direct quotations illustrating key points were noted. In two instances (noted in the text) material which was unique to single respondents is used: one of these two respondents was an Asian woman, the second had been in foster care throughout most of her childhood. While this 'low number' data is difficult to manage, ignoring it would have done further disservice to respondents in minority groups. Qualitative analysis is full of pitfalls, and it might be claimed this study tripped into a number of them (see Mason 1996 for a useful guide). Nonetheless, the themes selected reflected the concerns and experiences of the students and given that there has been hardly any such material published before, I make no apologies for its limitations. All the students names, with the exception of Jason Awbery-Taylor, have been changed in the body of the book. Those who specifically requested acknowledgement by name are listed at the beginning of the book.

Before embarking on the research I held discussions with the University Counselling Service and the Disabled Students Resource Unit in case the nature of the study touched on difficult areas which the researcher was unable to address, or where it would have been inappropriate to try. By working with the university services on this project, we were able to negotiate in advance an appropriate follow-up by them for any students raising new issues, or inadvertently distressed by the process of the research. While it was clearly no part of our plans to cause distress, interviewing young people about personal issues invariably carries such risks, and we were anxious to ensure that they would be supported should this happen. Happily, there proved to be no need.

The book also refers to other research projects:

The Waterside Project, the findings from which are published in *Child and Family Social Work* **3**, (3) 1998, addressed questions about the appropriate focus and direction of social work with disabled children, by linking parental views with those of social workers. Parents of nine disabled children were interviewed after the introduction of a specialist disability team in an inner city borough, following the implementation of the Children Act 1989. The interviews took place over a nine month period in 1995, and the comments of parents were then shared with social workers both from the borough concerned and from elsewhere.

Voluntary Sector Research, published in *Disability and Society* **14**, (1) 1999 involved a case study of a local project run by a national voluntary organisation which provides services for disabled children and their families. The project was set up in 1988 with joint funding; research was conducted over a six month period during 1996/7. The aim of the study was to explore the changing nature of the relationships between the voluntary organisation and the local social services department, and to identify specific issues for voluntary organisations regarding the contracting out of services for disabled children. Semi-structured interviews were conducted with staff from the voluntary organisation, including social workers, a play and leisure co-ordinator, outreach workers and the manager. In social services, similar interviews were held with senior managers, the Special Needs (operational) manager, and field social workers who specialised in working with disabled children and their families. The researcher also spent time with those children and families using the project. In addition, other voluntary organisations who were listed in the local Council for Voluntary Service were contacted by telephone.

Professional Network (an ongoing project). The author has brought together a network of social workers with disabled children over the last four years. This group meets three times a year to discuss issues around service provision for disabled children, and is a source of information about developments in 19 local authorities. In addition to the discussions, members have completed a number of questionnaires, been the subjects of more detailed interviewing and helped with access to service users.

Appendix 2

Letter to Social Exclusion Unit

Social Exclusion Unit
Cabinet Office
First Floor
Government Offices
Great George Street
LONDON
SW1P 3AL

26th February 1998

FAX 0171 270 1971

Dear Sir/Madam

Social Exclusion Unit

I very much welcome the Government's initiatives in setting up this Unit, and look forward to watching its progress.

I am currently working on a book for Blackwell Science about services for disabled children, and would very much like to include information on the Government's plans to tackle the discrimination they continue to experience in much of our health and welfare system.

I am sure that having David Blunkett at the DFEE will mean their needs will be considered in his reforms there, but I have found that much of the thinking on the exclusion of disabled children ... [and the European Commission is an example of this] ... does not go much further than their educational needs.

I appreciate these are early days and that you have a great deal of work ahead of you, and I therefore have no wish to burden you with a long letter, although I am happy to provide more information if desired!

I would be grateful for details of any plans, proposals or policy documents you have available, and if possible the name of any member of the Unit with a particular interest in tackling the exclusion of disabled children.

Best Wishes,

Laura Middleton
Head of Social Work
University of Central Lancashire

Appendix 3

The Process of Assessment

(1) Establishing a working relationship
- I   establishing a means of communication
- II   timing it
- III establishing groundrules
- IV   acknowledging feelings.

(2) Data collection
- I   aspirations: what the individual wants
- II   barriers/problems/stresses
- III resources/sources of support
- IV   coping mechanisms
- V   expert evidence.

(3) Analysis
- I   what the individual wants
- II   identifying changes which are required
- III identifying risks
- IV   identifying opportunities
- V   identifying the role of service providers
- VI   costing
- VII weighing up the options.

(4) Planning
- I   draft proposals
- II   negotiation
- III recommendations
- IV   arrangements for review
- V   ensuring quality.

This is adapted from *The Art of Assessment* (Middleton, 1997a) where a more detailed description of the process can be found.

References

Allen, J. (1996) Foucault and special educational needs: a 'Box of Tools' for analysing children's experiences of mainstreaming *Disability and Society* 11(2) 219–33.

American Academy of Pediatricians (1982) Policy Statement: the Doman-Delacato treatment of neurologically handicapped children. *Pediatrics* 70, 810–12.

Anonymous (1997) 'Student Mess Up' Letter to *Rubber Glove*, pre-registration student nurses newspaper, University of Central Lancashire, Preston, 2, (2) (pages not numbered).

Audit Commission (1994) *Seen but not heard: co-ordinating community child health and social services for children in need*. London, HMSO.

Audit Commission (1998) 'Working towards Best Value' *Headlines Newsletter* Summer 1998. Abingdon, Audit Commission Publications.

Awbery-Taylor, J. (1994) 'My Life in their Hands,' unpublished autobiography.

Balarajan, R. & Botting, B. (1989) Perinatal mortality in England and Wales; variations by mother's country of birth (1982–85). *Health Trends* 211, 79–84.

Baldwin, S.M. (1985) *The Costs of Caring: Families with Disabled Children*. London, Routledge & Kegan Paul.

Bamford, D., Griffiths, H., Long, S. & Kernochan, G. (1997) Analysis of consumer satisfaction in cerebral palsy care. *Journal of Inter-professional care* 11, 187–93.

Banim, M. & Guy, A. (1995) 'Peer sex education with disabled people'. Unpublished paper, Social Aspects of Aids Conference, London. Quoted in *The Sexual Politics of Disability: Untold Desires* (1996) (eds) T. Shakespeare, K. Gillespie-Sells & D. Davies, London, Cassell.

Bannister, A., Barrett, K. & Shearer, E. (eds) (1997) *Listening to Children: The Professional Response to Hearing the Abused Child*. London, Wiley/NSPCC.

Barnes, C. (1994) *Disabled People in Britain and Discrimination* (2nd Edn.). London, Hurst & Co.

Barron, K. (1997) The Bumpy Road to Womanhood *Disability and Society* 12 (2), 223–39.

Barstow, P., Cochrane, R. & Hur, J. (1993) *Evaluation of Conductive Education for Children with Cerebral Palsy*. DFE/University of Birmingham.

Bax, M.C.O. (1993) Conductive Education assessed. *Dev. Med. Child Neurology*, 35 659–60.

Beresford, B. (1994) Positively parents: caring for a severely disabled child *SPRU Papers*. London, HMSO.

Beresford, B. (1995) *Expert Opinions: a survey of parents caring for a severely disabled child*. Bristol, Policy Press.

Beresford, B., Sloper, P., Baldwin, S.M. & Newman, T. (1996) *What works in services for families with a disabled child?* Essex, Barnardo's.

Bleck, E. (1987) *Orthopaedic Management of Cerebral Palsy*. Oxford, Blackwell Science.

Boateng, P. (1997) 'Taking responsibility and giving control' Interview to *Children's Services News*. Department of Health, July 1997.

Brown, L., Long, E., Udvari-Solner, A. *et al.* (1989) The home school: why students with severe intellectual disabilities must attend the schools of their brothers, sisters, friends, and neighbours. *Journal of the Association for Persons with Severe Handicaps* **14**, 1–7.

Butler, I. (1998) Used and abused: engaging the child in child protection in *Engaging the User in Welfare Services* (eds) A. Pithouse & H. Williamson. Birmingham, Venture Press.

Byrne, E.A. & Cunningham, C.C. (1985) The effects of mentally handicapped children on families – a conceptual review. *Journal of Child Psychology and Psychiatry* **26**, 847–64.

Cabinet Office (1997) *Social Exclusion Unit: purpose, work priorities and working methods* (Leaflet). London, Cabinet Office.

Campbell, J. & Oliver, M. (1996) *Disability Politics: understanding our past, changing our future*. London, Routledge.

Campling, J. (1981) (ed) *Images of Ourselves*. London, Routledge & Kegan Paul.

Casey, K. (1994) *Teaching Children with Special Needs*. Wentworth Falls, Social Science Press.

Channer, Y. & Parton, P. (1990) Racism, cultural relativism and child protection. In *Violence against Children Study Group: Taking Child Abuse Seriously*, pp 105–20. London and New York, Unwin.

Chaudary, V. (1997) Man who killed disabled daughter escapes mandatory life term, *Guardian*, 2 December 1998.

Children Act (England and Wales) (1989) London, HMSO.

Churchill, J., Craft, A., Holding A. & Horrocks C. (1993) (eds) *It could never happen here! The prevention and treatment of sexual abuse of adults with learning disabilities in residential settings*. DoH/SSI/ARC/NAPSAC.

Cooper, C. (1997) Can a fat woman call herself disabled? *Disability and Society* **12** (1), 31–41.

Cumming, R.A. (1988) *The Neurologically-impaired Child: Doman-Delacato Techniques Re-appraised*. London, Croom-Helm.

Dartington Social Research Unit (1995) *Child Protection: Messages from Research*. London, HMSO.

Daunt, P. (1996) Disability and the European Community: Sources of Initiative. In P. Mittler & V. Sinason (eds), *Changing Policy and Practice for People with Learning Disabilities*. London, Cassell Education.

Department of Education and Science (1978) *Special Educational Needs: DES/ Welsh Office Consultative Document*. London, HMSO [The Warnock Report].

Department of Education (1989) *A report by HMI Inspectors: Provision for Primary-Aged Pupils with Statements of Special Educational Needs in Mainstream Schools.* London, DES.

Department of Health (1990) *Caring for People: Community Care in the Next Decade and Beyond.* London, HMSO.

Department of Health (1994) *Children Act Report 1993.* London, HMSO.

Department of Health (1996) *The National Health Service: A Service with Ambitions.* Cmd 3425, London. HMSO.

Department of Health (1997a) *Social Services – Achievement and Challenge* London, HMSO.

Department of Health (1997b) *The New NHS: Modern, Dependable.* Cmd 3807 London, HMSO.

Department of Health (1998) *Modernising Social Services.* Cmd 4169, London, HMSO.

Department of Health/Social Services Inspectorate (1991) *Care Management and Assessment: Practitioner's Guide.* London, HMSO.

Department of Health/DFEE (1997) *Children's Service Planning: Guidance.* London, HMSO.

Dickerson, J.W.T., Tingle, P.A., Barrington P. & Pennock J.K. (1987) Development of Brain Injured Children *The Journal of the Royal Society of Health* **107**, 115–23.

Dunn, L.M. (1968) Special education for mentally retarded – is much of it justifiable? *Exceptional Children* **35**, 5–22.

Durham County Council (1996) *Integrating Children: A Consultation Document.* Durham County Council.

Durham County Council Social Services (1997) *Managing the Future. Services for Children and Families.* Durham County Council.

Dyson, A. & Gains, C. (1995) The Role of the Special Needs Co-ordinator: Poisoned Chalice or Crock of Gold. *Support for Learning* **10** (2).

Eastwood, M. (1998) 'Defining Issues' *Guardian*, 4 March 1998.

Eley, R. & Middleton, L. (1983) Square Pegs, Round holes? The appropriateness of providing care for old people in residential settings. *Health Trends* **15**(3,) 68–70.

European Commission (1995) *The Evaluation of HELIOS II: Interim Report.* Luxembourg, Office for Official Publications of the European Communities V/6823/95.

European Commission (1996a) *The Evaluation of HELIOS II.* Brussels 23 January 1996 Com (96) 8 final.

European Commission (1996b) *Communication of the Commission on Equality of Opportunity for People with Disabilities.* Brussels, 30 July 1996 COM(96)406 final 96/0216.

European Commission (1996c) *Helios II European Guide of Good Practice: Towards Equal Opportunities for Disabled People.* Luxembourg, Office for Official Publications of the European Communities.

Fay, T. (1953) Evaluation of basic patterns of movements in man; their diagnostic significance in spinal paralysis. *Arch Neurol Psychiatry* **69**, 530.

Flanaghan, J. (1997) Letter to the *Guardian* 28 October 1998.

Flynn, M. with Liverpool Self Advocates (1994) *Taking a Break.* Manchester, National Development Team.

Ford, J. (1982) *Special Education and Social Control*. London, Routledge & Kegan Paul.

French, S. (1998) 'The wind gets in my way': Discourse and Visual Disability, in S. French & M. Corker (1998) (Eds) *Disability Discourse*. Buckingham, Open University Press.

Gardner, R. (1998) *Family Support*. Birmingham, Venture Press.

Garnett, J. (1996) Changing Classroom Practice. In P. Mitre & V. Sinason (eds) *Changing Policy and Practice for People with Learning Disabilities*. London, Cassell Education.

Glendinning, C. (1983) *Unshared Care: Parents and their Disabled Children*. London, Routledge & Kegan Paul.

Goldring, M. (1998) *Cradle to Grave: Rationing in the NHS*. Channel 4 television programme, June 1998.

Graves, P., (1993) Categorica. *British Medical Journal* 307, 4 September 1993, p 630–31.

Graves, P., (1995) Therapy Methods for cerebral palsy *Journal Paediatric Child Health* 31, 24–8.

Harding, L. (1998) Children's Rights, in O. Stevenson (ed), *Child Welfare in the UK*. Oxford, Blackwell Science.

Heaton, M. (1998) Listen, you might hear something! *Outlook* 15, June 1998, p 12.

Hegarty, S. (1982) Meeting special education needs in the ordinary school. *Educational Research* 24, 174–81.

Hegarty S. (1987) *Meeting Special Needs in Ordinary Schools*. London, Cassell Education.

Hirst, M.A. (1991) Dissolution and reconstitution of families with a disabled young person. *Developmental Medicine and Child Neurology*, 33, 1073–9.

Hirst, M.A. & Baldwin, S.M. (1994) Unequal Opportunities: Growing up Disabled, *SPRU Papers*. London, HMSO.

Hopkins, A. & Bahl, V. (1993) (eds) *Access to health care for people from black and ethnic minorities*. London, Royal College of Physicians.

Hornby, G., (1995) The Code of Practice: Boon or Burden? *British Journal of Special Education* 22 (3) 116–19.

Humphreys, S. & Gordon, P. (1992) *Out of Sight: The Experience of Disability 1900–1950*. Plymouth, Northcote House.

James, A. (1994) *Managing to Care: Public Service and the Market*. London, Longman.

Jay, P. (1996) Exodus: Bringing children out of hospital in P. Mittler & V. Sinason (eds) *Changing Policy and Practice for People with Learning Disabilities*. London, Cassell Education.

Jonsson, T. (1994) *Inclusive Education*. Geneva, United Nations Development Programme.

Keith, L. (ed) (1994) *Mustn't Grumble: Writings by Disabled Women*. London, Women's Press.

Kelly, L. (1992) The connections between disability and child abuse: a review of the research evidence. *Child Abuse Review* 1(3), 157–67.

Kennedy, M. (1989) The abuse of deaf children *Child Abuse Review*, 3 (1) 3–7.

Kennedy, M. (1990) The deaf child who is sexually abused – is there a need for a dual specialist? *Child Abuse Review*, 4 (2) 3–6.

Kennedy, M. (1996) Sexual Abuse and Disabled Children, in J. Morris (ed) *Encounters with Strangers*, London, Women's Press.

Knight, A. (1998) *Valued or Forgotten?* London, National Children's Bureau.

Knipe, H. & Maclay, G. (1973) *The Dominant Man: The pecking order in human society*. London, Fontana/Collins.

Kurtz, Z. (1993) Better health for black and ethnic minority children and young people, in A. Hopkins & V. Bahl (eds), *Access to health care for people from black and ethnic minorities*. London, Royal College of Physicians.

Lewis, A. (1995) *Children's Understanding of Disability*. London, Routledge.

Lister, R. (1990) *The Exclusive Society: citizenship and the poor*. London, Child Poverty Action Group.

Lumb, K., Congdon, P. & Lealman, G. (1981) A comparative review of Asian and British born maternity patients in Bradford, 1974–78, *Journal of Epidemiology and Community Health* 35, 106–9.

Marchant, R. & Page, M. (1992) *Bridging the Gap*. London, NSPCC.

Marfo, K. & Kysela, G. (1985) Early intervention with mentally handicapped children: A critical appraisal of applied research. *Journal of Paediatric Psychology* 1985 (10) 305–24.

Mason, J. (1996) *Qualitative Researching* London, Sage Publications.

Middleton, L. (1996) *Making a Difference: Social Work with Disabled Children*. Birmingham, Venture Press.

Middleton, L. (1997a) *The Art of Assessment*. Birmingham, Venture Press.

Middleton, L. (1997b) 'All the Running you can do...' Keynote address to NAPSAC Annual Conference, Nottingham, 2 October 1977.

Middleton L. (1998a) 'Services for disabled children'. Paper to 2nd International Conference on Social Work in Health and Mental Health, Melbourne, January 1998.

Middleton L. (1998b) Consumer satisfaction with services for disabled children, *Journal of Interprofessional Care* 12 (2) 223–31.

Middleton, L. (1998c) Services for disabled children: integrating the perspective of the social workers, *Child and Family Social Work* 3, 239–46.

Middleton, L. (1999) The Social Exclusion of Disabled Children: the role of the Voluntary Sector in the Contract Culture, *Disability and Society* 14(1), 129–39.

Miller, R. & Murphy, D. (1998) *Social Work and HIV/Aids*. Birmingham, Venture Press.

Morris, J. (1991) *Pride Against Prejudice*. London, Women's Press.

Morris, J. (1996a) *Gone Missing? A research and policy review of disabled children living away from their families*. London, Who Cares Trust.

Morris, J. (ed) (1996b) *Encounters with Strangers: Feminism and Disability*. London, Women's Press.

Morris, J. (1997) Gone missing? Disabled children living away from their families, *Disability and Society* 2 (2), April 1997, 241–58.

Moseley, J. (1994) Developing Self Esteem, *Special Children* (Back to Basics insert) 12, (74), 1–8.

Mullender, A. (1996) *Rethinking Dometic Violence: the Social Work and Probation Response*. London, Routledge.

Muthukrishna A. (1996) 'The inclusion of children with Down's syndrome into mainstream schools: A South African experience.' Program and abstracts of

10th World Congress of the International Association for the Scientific Study of Intellectual Disabilities. Helsinki, July 1996.

National Health and Medical Research Council (1993) *Report on Conductive Education and its Applicability in Australia*. Canberra, Australian Government Publishing Service.

National Union of Teachers (1995) *Survey on Pupil Exclusions. Information to LEAs*. London, NUT.

NHS Executive (1998) *Signposts for Success in Commissioning and Providing Health Services for people with Learning Disabilities*. London, Department of Health.

NSPCC (1993) ABCD: *ABuse of Children who are Disabled*. Training and Resource Pack, London, NSPCC.

Oliver, M. (1990) *The Politics of Disablement* London, MacMillan.

Oliver, M. (1994) Does Special Education have a role to play in the Twenty First Century? Keynote Address at the Sixth Annual Conference on Special Education, IATSE, Dublin. In *REACH, Journal of Special Needs Education In Ireland*, 8 (2), (1995), 67–76.

Oppenheim, C. & Harker, L. (1996) *Poverty: The Facts*, London, Child Poverty Action Group.

Orbach, S. (1997) 'A culture of child hating', *Guardian Weekend*. 4th January 1997.

Parton, N. (1997) Current Debates and Future Prospects: in N. Parton (ed) *Child Protection and Family Support: tensions, contradictions and possibilities*. London, Routledge.

Patel, K. (1993) Ethnic minority access to services, in J. Harrison (ed) *Race, Culture and Substance Problems*. University of Hull.

Pennock, K. (1991) *Rescuing Brain Injured Children*. Bath, Ashgrove Press.

Plummer, K. (1995) *Telling Sexual Stories*. London, Routledge.

Prejean, H. (1993) *Dead Man Walking*. London, Fount.

Priestley, M. (1998a) Childhood disability and disabled childhoods: agendas for research. *Childhood* 5 (2), 207–23.

Priestley, M. (1998b) Discourse and identity: disabled children in mainstream high schools, in S. French & M. Corker (1998) (eds) *Disability Discourse*. Buckingham, Open University Press.

Randall, P. (1997) *Adult Bullying: Perpetrators and Victims*. London, Routledge.

Roberts, J. & Taylor, C. (1993) Sexually Abused Children and Young People Speak Out, in L. Waterhouse (ed) *Child Abuse and Child Abusers: Protection and Prevention*. London, Jessica Kingsley.

Robinson, C. (1987) *Taking a Break: A study of Respite Care for Families Living in Bristol and Weston Health District*. Bristol, University of Bristol.

Royal College of Paediatrics and Child Health (1997) *A multi-disciplinary Appraisal of the British Institute for Brain Injured Children (BIBIC) 1995–1997*. London, British Association for Community Child Health.

Runnymede Trust (1997) *Islamophobia: a challenge for us all*. London, Runnymede Trust.

Russell, P. (1994) *The Children Act 1989: Children and Young People with Learning Disabilities: Some Opportunities and Challenges*. Manchester, National Development Team.

Searing, H. (1998) Times Change, Values Don't, *Professional Social Work*. February 1998.

Secretary of State for Social Services (1988) *Report of the Inquiry into Child Abuse in Cleveland*. Cmd 412, London, HMSO.

Shakespeare, T.W. & Watson, N. (1998) Theoretical perspectives on Research with Disabled Children, in C. Robinson & K. Stalker, (eds), *Growing Up with Disability*. London, Jessica Kingsley.

Shakespeare, T., Gillespie-Sells, K. & Davies, D. (1996) *The Sexual Politics of Disability: Untold Desires*. London, Cassell.

Sloper, P. & Turner, S. (1992) Service needs of families of children with severe physical disability, *Childcare, Health and Development*. 18, 259–82.

Smith, R. (1992) Poor Britain: Losing Out, *British Medical Journal* 305 (1).

Social Services Inspectorate/Department of Health (1994) *Services for Disabled Children: report of the national inspection of services to disabled children and their families*. London, HMSO.

Sparrow, S. & Ziegler, E. (1978) Evaluation of patterning treatment for retarded children, *Pediatrics* 62, 137–50.

Stakes, J.R. (1996) *The Code of Practice: Some Preliminary Thoughts from Teachers*. Doncaster College, Occasional Papers.

Stakes, J.R., & Hornby, G. (1997) *Change in Special Education*. London, Cassell.

Stainback, W. & Stainback, S. (eds) (1994) *Support Networks for Inclusive Schooling*. Baltimore, Paul H. Brookes.

Stalker, K. (1990) *Share the Care: An evaluation of a family based respite scheme*. London, Jessica Kingsley.

Stalker, K. & Robinson, C. (1991) *Out of Touch: the Non-users of Respite Care Services*. Bristol, University of Bristol.

Stevenson, O. (1997) '50 years of services to children in need of care: What have we learnt for tomorrow?' Lucy Faithful Memorial Lecture, St Anne's College, Oxford, 15 March 1997.

Stevenson, O. (1998) *Neglected Children: issues and dilemmas*. Oxford, Blackwell Science.

Swain, J., French, S. & Gillman, M. (1998), *Confronting Disabling Barriers: towards making organisations accessible*. Birmingham, Venture Press.

Thomas, H. (1998) 'Got you, teach', *Guardian* 28 July 1998.

Tomlinson, S. (1982) *A Sociology of Special Education*. London, Routledge & Kegan Paul.

Tomlinson, S. & Colquhoun, R. (1995) The Political Economy of Special Educational Needs in Britain, *Disability and Society* 10 (2), 191–202.

Toolis, K. (1996) 'A heart for Jo'. *Guardian Weekend* 10 August 1996.

Utting, W. (1997) *People Like Us: the report of the review of the safeguards for children living away from home*. London, DoH/HMSO.

Valletutti, P. (1969) Integration vs. segregation: a useless dialectic. *Journal of Special Education* 3, 405–8.

Vargo, R. & Vargo, J. (1995) Voice of inclusion: my friend, Ro Vargo. In R.A. Villa & J.S. Thousand (eds) *Creating an Inclusive School*. Alexandria, Association for Supervision and Development.

Veash, N. (1998) 'Down's child at centre of schooling row', *Independent on Sunday* 12 April 1998.

Vernon, A. (1996) A stranger in many camps: The experience of disabled and black minority ethnic women, in J. Morris (ed) *Encounters with Strangers: Feminism and Disability*. London, Women's Press.

Villa, R.A. & Thousand, J.S. (1995) (eds) *Creating an Inclusive School.* Alexandria, Association for Supervision and Development.

Wallace, M. & Robson, M. (1975) *On Giant's Shoulders: The Terry Wiles Story.* London, Times Books.

Wang, M.C., Walberg, H. & Reynolds, M.C. (1992) A scenario for better – not separate – special education, *Educational Leadership* 50, 35–8.

Ward, D. (1995) 'Court denies brain damage boy his choice of school', *Guardian* 28 October 1998.

Weale, J. & Bradshaw, J. (1980) Prevalence and characteristics of disabled children: findings from the 1974 General Household survey. *Journal of Epidemiology and Community Health* 34, 11–18.

Westcott, H.L. (1993) *Abuse of Children and Adults with Disabilities.* London, NSPCC.

Westcott, H.L. & Cross, M. (1995) *This Far and No Further: Toward Ending the Abuse of Disabled Children.* Birmingham, Venture Press.

Index